T0367950

Navy SEAL's Guide to Surviving Invasions, Civil War, and World War III

Navy SEAL's Guide to Surviving Invasions, Civil War, and World War III

Clint Emerson and H Keith Melton

Archway Publishing books may be ordered through booksellers or by contacting:

Archway Publishing
1663 Liberty Drive
Bloomington, IN 47403
www.archwaypublishing.com
844-669-3957

Because of the dynamic nature of the Internet, any web addresses or
links contained in this book may have changed since publication and
may no longer be valid. The views expressed in this work are solely those
of the author and do not necessarily reflect the views of the publisher,
and the publisher hereby disclaims any responsibility for them.

Any people depicted in stock imagery provided by Getty Images are
models, and such images are being used for illustrative purposes only.
Certain stock imagery © Getty Images.

Interior Graphics/Art Credit: David Regone

ISBN: 978-1-6657-5579-5 (sc)
ISBN: 978-1-6657-5580-1 (hc)
ISBN: 978-1-6657-5592-4 (e)

Library of Congress Control Number: 2024901967

Print information available on the last page.

Archway Publishing rev. date: 04/08/2024

A NOTE TO READERS

The skills featured in these pages were provided by special operations personnel and clandestine warfare specialists—a cadre of multidiscipline experts who have tested the limits of their intelligence, endurance, precision, and ingenuity under life-threatening conditions.

Collectively we have cobbled together basic soldiering skills, small unit tactics, special activities, and some tricks of the trade that are intended to assist anyone faced with defending their homeland. The resulting manual is intended to expose civilians to a variety of skill sets, weapons, and firearms used in combat. Some techniques have been specially adapted for small teams of resistance facing a range of deadly situations, from ambushes and snipers to being overrun by armored vehicles. The book's primary and intended purpose is educate and inform you how to save lives—yours and those of the people around you. Still, some of the skills are extremely dangerous and should only be attempted in the direst of situations when lives are at risk and there is no one to call for help. Safety precautions should always be taken.

All skills require the application of personal judgment and appropriateness for a given situation and are highly dependent on context. The authors, contributors, illustrator, and publisher disclaim any liability from any injury or damages of any type that may result from the use, proper or improper, or misuse of the information contained in this book. The stated goal of the book is not to enable or encourage survival during wartime but to entertain while simultaneously introducing a body of knowledge that may come in handy in the absolute direst of emergencies.

Be deadly in spirit but not in action (unless the actions against you are deadly). Don't do stupid things, *always* respect the rights of others, and obey the laws of the land. The strongest and best prepared are the ones who survive and fight back.

If someone comes to kill you, rise up and kill him first. (The Talmud)

For informational purposes only,
exercise caution, prioritize safety, and obey all laws.

v

LEGAL STUFF AND DISCLAIMER

The contents of this book are provided solely for informational and educational purposes. By engaging with this book, you acknowledge and agree to the following terms and conditions.

1. No Incitement or Endorsement: The authors, publisher, and distributor of this book do not endorse, promote, or incite any illegal, unsafe, or harmful activities. The information presented is intended to inform and educate readers but should never be misconstrued as an encouragement to engage in any unlawful or dangerous actions. **2. Personal Responsibility:** Every reader is solely responsible for their actions and decisions based on the information contained within this book. The authors, publisher, and distributor do not assume any liability for the consequences arising from the reader's use or misuse of the information provided. **3. Safety Precautions:** It is imperative to exercise extreme caution, sound judgment, and the highest regard for safety when applying any knowledge gained from this book. Safety should always be a paramount concern, and appropriate precautions must be taken to prevent harm to oneself or others. **4. Legal Compliance:** Readers must adhere to all relevant local, state, and national laws and regulations when considering and implementing any concepts or practices discussed in this book. This book does not advocate or condone actions that are in violation of the law. **5. No Substitute for Professional Advice:** This book does not substitute for professional guidance, medical advice, or legal counsel. For specific issues requiring expert knowledge or guidance, readers are strongly encouraged to consult with qualified professionals who are experts in their respective fields. **6. No Liability:** The authors, publisher, and distributor expressly disclaim any liability for any direct, indirect, incidental, consequential, or special damages that may arise from the use or reliance upon the information presented in this book. **7. Accuracy of Information:** While every effort has been made to ensure the accuracy and reliability of the information contained within this book, neither the authors, publisher, nor distributor make any warranties or representations regarding the completeness, accuracy, or suitability of the information for any particular purpose. **8. Assumption**

For informational purposes only,
exercise caution, prioritize safety, and obey all laws.

vii

of Risk: Readers are presumed to have assumed all risks associated with using the information provided in this book, and they shall hold harmless the authors, publisher, and distributor from any claims arising from such use. **9. Professional Consultation:** For critical matters involving health, safety, legal issues, or other complex areas, readers are strongly advised to seek advice from qualified professionals who can provide expert guidance tailored to their specific circumstances. **10. Acceptance of Terms:** If you disagree with any part of this disclaimer, return your book immediately for a full refund. By reading this book, you acknowledge and accept the terms outlined in this disclaimer.

INTRODUCTION

Citizen soldiers engage in organized actions against foreign invaders and host governments gone rogue. Whether the threat is external, such as the invading army of a neighboring country, or internal, such as the infiltration of a Marxist/Leninist regime, your life and your way of life are in danger. The likely outcome of both types of threats is that human rights will quickly disappear and cherished democratic values will be tossed to the gutter to achieve a "worker's paradise" and socialist utopia.

Unfortunately, such dangers are no longer confined to far-flung locations and seem to be inching closer and closer to our shores each year. Acts of terror, mass shootings, riots, lawlessness, public disorder, rampant crime, and chaos are no longer by-products of war zones and unstable countries and have impacted neighborhoods much closer to home.

In a not-too-distant future where every stranger poses a potential threat, understanding the mindset of the invader or predator provides you with a small advantage. Understanding the techniques that may be employed against you prepares you for the uncertain world that may lie ahead. Can you spot an ambush? Do you know how to take out a tank using only the ingredients available in your household? What are the techniques used in recent history to confront larger and better-armed invading armies? Once your country is about to be invaded, however, it is likely too late to begin an inquiry. Or you can begin now to learn the necessary skills you may need from some of the most highly trained specialists on the planet.

Facing armed invaders or rogue governments requires more preparations than a storage closet filled with canned peas and bottles of distilled water. The skills in this book were adapted from the world of special operations and clandestine warfare, a complex web of associations dominated by operatives with combat experience and a shared predilection for intrigue and danger. As highly skilled warriors, they have risked their lives in conflicts and war zones around the world. Their very survival has depended on them mastering the skills of spies, soldiers, and lawbreakers.

While some of the techniques used in special operations warfare could not be shown in this book without endangering public safety, many highly useful techniques can be shared that may save your life and those that you love. Each skill is broken down into its most complex parts, or Courses of Action (COAs), and summed up by a BLUFF (Bottom Line Up Front), which spells out the key takeaway from the operative's perspective; some skills can also be reversed to outline preventative measures fighters can take the arm themselves against invaders or predators employing these techniques.

As a retired Navy SEAL who's been several years inside the National Security Agency (NSA), in writing this book, Clint Emerson drew on a range of experience that spans more than twenty years running special ops all over the world, both in teams and alone, and merges lessons learned from both combat and surveillance.

H. Keith Melton is a graduate of the US Naval Academy (Class of 1966), Vietnam combat veteran, prolific author, and recognized internationally as an authority on clandestine tradecraft. Emerson and Melton first worked together on projects at NSA and in 2015 jointly created the concept for "100 Deadly Skills." Over these last nine years, the world has become progressively more dangerous, and they are pleased to join forces again.

The skills in this book represent a potential path for resistance in a variety of different situations—whether you're facing invaders from a neighboring country, a host government gone rogue, or street violence run amok. Learning how to think like a citizen soldier and protect yourself will significantly improve your chances of coming out on top.

1
BASIC SOLDIERING SKILLS

ANATOMY OF A
CITIZEN SOLDIER

The phrase "The British are coming!" is attributed to Paul Revere, a colonial Boston silversmith and patriot who was among several riders who sounded the alarm that the British regulars were coming to attack the American colonies. On the night of April 18, 1775, Revere and William Dawes set out on horseback from Boston to warn the colonists that the British were planning to march on Concord to seize American military supplies. Revere rode through the countryside, waking sleeping towns and farms while shouting his famous warning: "The British are coming! The British are coming!" This remains an iconic symbol of American rebellion and a war cry to all American citizen soldiers.

Citizen soldiers defend themselves and their homeland against a numerically superior and better-armed invading force or host governments and dictatorships gone crazy. While they might be outgunned in larger battles, citizen soldiers can create an advantage over the invaders in smaller encounters with an intimate knowledge of the countryside, time to prepare defenses, and support from the local population.

The most critical mindset for a citizen soldier is preparation and relentless awareness of the threats to his or her homeland. Today's civilian is tomorrow's citizen soldier, and you can begin training to learn the necessary skills. From marksmanship to field craft, camouflage, disguise, covert communications, cybersafety, escape routes, navigation, etc., the time to start learning is now.

While citizen soldiers are more efficient and effective operating in five-person teams, they also need the skills to operate alone. Crossing borders, escaping and evading, eliminating high-value targets, and blending back into the population may involve solo skills and a sophisticated risk assessment and analytical aptitude. In our increasingly dangerous world, civilians who become well-versed in the skills discussed in this book will have an advantage over the general population if the need arises.

Citizen soldiers actively defending their cities on the front lines have

No. 001: The Citizen Soldier

CONOP: Distribute and conceal escape and survival tools to lessen the risk of being caught.

RURAL

- Combat shovel
- Balaclava
- Pack
- CS marking
- Concealed Pistol
- Fixed blade
- Boots
- Extra magazines
- Scar concealment
- Razor blade

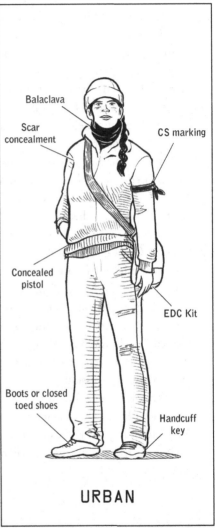

URBAN

- Balaclava
- Scar concealment
- CS marking
- Concealed pistol
- EDC Kit
- Boots or closed toed shoes
- Handcuff key

BLUF: Dress to avoid scrutiny and blend-in with your surroundings.

For informational purposes only,
exercise caution, prioritize safety, and obey all laws.

little expectation or need for anonymity and may freely carry and employ their weaponry. However, sabotage operations in occupied areas often require specialized gear, and to remain undetected among the general population, you must learn to become anonymous.

Some skills in this book are attuned to living and operating in an occupied area, while others become more relevant in urban combat.

Survival inside occupied areas requires that citizen soldiers blend into their surroundings. A carefully managed appearance allows them to avoid detection by both potential witnesses and the occupier's security service. Clothing should not appear distinctive and never attract curiosity or scrutiny. Beyond being unremarkable, sometimes their clothing must conceal the equipment needed for an operation and an escape. The key is always to blend in.

Citizen soldiers must learn to adapt and overcome obstacles using improvised tools and equipment. While fictional spies employ multiple fanciful devices and high-tech toys in their daring adventures, in the real world, each gadget becomes a liability if it can't be explained and justified when stopped and questioned. However, improvised solutions can be crafted. One example: Mobile phones can be eavesdropped on and tracked unless you improvise a Faraday cage from an old metal ammunition box to make signals "go dark" and become invisible to snoopers.

In the cyber age, communications have become a necessary liability. However, citizen soldiers understand that all cybercommunications are insecure and avoid leaving digital breadcrumbs that can be tracked and targeted. Low-tech or no-tech options are always preferred if you can accomplish the mission.

The wartime skills in this book are presented to stop an invading army or a host government gone rogue. Though some of the techniques are helpful in peacetime, others may be unlawful and are presented only for informational purposes. Use common sense, and obey the laws in your country.

EVERYDAY CARRY (EDC)

The term *everyday carry (EDC) items* refers to a set of essential items that people carry with them every day. These items are meant to be useful in various situations, from an invasion to personal emergencies or everyday tasks, depending on the individual's job, lifestyle, and environment. Having EDC items can be crucial in the event of unexpected emergencies or life-threatening situations. To maintain a state of constant preparedness, citizen soldiers may need to carry different types of EDC items. Each will be configured to address expected threats, such as supporting missions or self-rescue specific. The items also provide an edge against unexpected threats.

One of the main reasons for having EDC items is to be prepared for eventualities that can happen at any time. For instance, imagine being stuck in a traffic jam, a sudden power outage, or having car trouble while on a road trip. Having EDC items like a flashlight, a pocketknife, a tire gauge, or a phone charger handy can make all the difference in these situations.

EDC items can also provide a sense of security and safety. Items like a whistle, pepper spray, or a personal alarm can help to draw attention in an emergency, deter attackers, or signal for help when needed.

Moreover, having EDC items can save time and increase efficiency in daily tasks. For instance, a pen, a notepad, a multitool, or a USB drive can be invaluable for staying organized and productive on the job. Having everyday carry items is important because it provides a sense of preparedness and readiness to handle unexpected situations or emergencies that may arise. It can also increase safety and efficiency while performing daily tasks. Therefore, it's essential to choose the right EDC items that suit your lifestyle, environment, and potential threats.

No. 002: Every Day Carry Kits

CONOP: Make sure life support and survival tools are concealed, but easy to access quickly when needed.

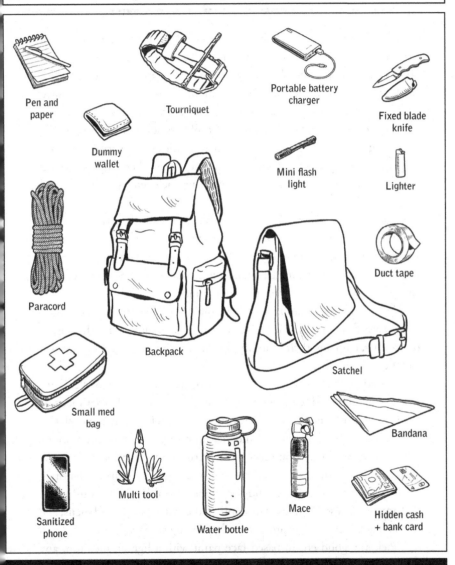

Pen and paper

Dummy wallet

Tourniquet

Portable battery charger

Fixed blade knife

Mini flash light

Lighter

Paracord

Backpack

Satchel

Duct tape

Bandana

Small med bag

Sanitized phone

Multi tool

Water bottle

Mace

Hidden cash + bank card

BLUF: Making it a lifestyle may save your life.

For informational purposes only,
exercise caution, prioritize safety, and obey all laws.

FACE CAMOUFLAGE

Face camouflage is an essential aspect of your military gear and preparations for the battlefield. Camouflage is a technique that helps to conceal military personnel from their enemies and makes them less visible to their opponents. The use of face camouflage is a fundamental aspect of this tactic and provides many benefits for citizen soldiers in combat.

Face camouflage can help to protect soldiers' identities from enemies, including drones, who may use facial recognition for surveillance and targeting. Providing an element of ambiguity in a soldier's appearance can offer a significant advantage by complicating the enemy's ability to track them effectively.

Face camouflage can help soldiers blend in with their surroundings, making them almost invisible in the right conditions. Soldiers can use natural materials like mud or charcoal to create the right camouflage for the environment. This can help make it much easier to remain hidden from the enemy, which can prevent potential attacks.

Face camouflage can help soldiers maintain their stealth and protect themselves from enemy snipers. Camouflage can help disrupt the outline of a soldier, reducing their visibility and making it much harder for snipers to take a shot at them.

Additionally, the use of face camouflage can contribute to alleviating soldiers' anxiety and fear, enabling them to maintain a sharper focus on their mission. When soldiers are aware that they are effectively camouflaged, it instills a sense of security, confidence, and improved concentration on their objectives. Face camouflage plays a crucial role in military gear and preparations on the battlefield, serving to safeguard soldiers' identities, merge them with their surroundings, uphold stealth, and minimize fear and anxiety. These advantages promote soldier safety, enhanced focus, and ultimately heighten their prospects of achieving success.

Pick any good cream-based face paint with a lighter, medium, and darker color. In a pinch, you can use charcoal and dirt/mud to achieve a similar effect. Warning: while shoe polish is effective for camouflage and comes in a variety of colors, it is very difficult to remove.

No. 003: Face Camouflage

CONOP: Facial camouflage is as essential as concealing your clothing and weapon.

COA1: Paint a 1.5" wide diagonal stripe with your darkest color across your face.

COA2: On both sides of the dark stripe add a similar stripe of your lightest color.

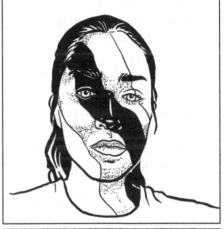

COA3: Use your darkest color again to fill in the remaining outside areas, including your neck and ears.

COA4: If you aren't wearing a hat and are bald, paint your entire head area.

BLUF: You can either blend-in or become a target.

For informational purposes only,
exercise caution, prioritize safety, and obey all laws.

GHILLIE BLANKET

A ghillie blanket is an essential piece of military gear that can be the difference between life and death on the battlefield. It is a type of camouflage cover that is designed to conceal military personnel and equipment from enemies.

The primary purpose of a ghillie blanket is to provide soldiers with effective camouflage. It can help soldiers quickly blend into their surroundings, making them less visible to the enemy. The ghillie blanket is made of natural materials like burlap, jute, and twine that are attached to the cover. This construction allows soldiers to blend into the terrain effectively, making it harder for them to be spotted by enemy forces.

In addition to camouflage, the ghillie blanket can also protect soldiers from harsh weather conditions. It can help keep soldiers warm during cold nights, protect them from wind and rain, and provide comfort when resting.

Another advantage of the ghillie blanket is that it can be used to create an improvised shelter on the battlefield. The natural materials used in its construction can be used to create a makeshift tent or shelter that can provide soldiers with protection from the elements.

Moreover, the ghillie blanket can also be used to cover and conceal equipment. Soldiers can cover their weapons and other personal equipment to make them less visible to the enemy. This ensures that they can move in stealth without being spotted by enemy forces. The ghillie blanket is an essential piece of military gear in combat. It provides soldiers with an effective camouflage solution, protection from harsh weather, a comfortable place to rest, and an improvised shelter on the battlefield. Its versatility and practicality make it an indispensable piece of equipment for modern-day soldiers who engage in direct combat.

No. 004: Ghillie Blanket

CONOP: Use the versatile camouflaged Ghillie Blanket to reduce the visual signature of a citizen and his equipment.

COA1: Drape the netting around your head to mark the hood and identify the spot for shoulder and waist ties.

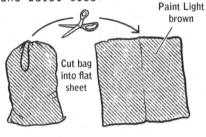

Paint Light brown

Cut bag into flat sheet

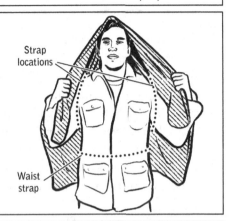

Strap locations

Waist strap

COA2: Add 24 foliage anchors (12" long) made from gutless 550 cord to the back of the net.

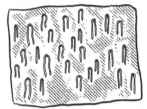

COA3: Tie burlap strips to the back of the blanket.

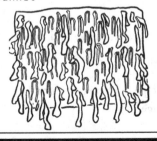

Use foliage to blend in with your environment or to hide gear.

For informational purposes only,
exercise caution, prioritize safety, and obey all laws.

NO. 005

RIFLE CAMOUFLAGE

Black is not a naturally occurring color in nature, and adversaries realize that most angular black objects on the battlefield are man-made and likely to be weapons. Fortunately, by eliminating the three main camouflage violations—glare, unnatural colors, and contrast with the background—your rifle can hide in plain sight. Effective weapon camouflage is always dependent on your operating environment and falls into three general scenarios: rural (foliage), snow (white), and urban.

For rural and urban surroundings, begin with heavy-duty rubber bands and burlap. Old sandbags work well when they are cut open.

1. Cut sections of burlap and wrap around your rifle's handguards, buttstock, and optics.
2. Secure the burlap with heavy-duty rubber bands.
3. In rural areas, attach fist-size clumps of local vegetation using the rubber bands.
4. For urban areas, cut two-inch by twelve-inch strips of burlap and attach them beneath the rubber bands. Fraying the edges of the burlap adds to their concealment.

In a white, snowy environment, a black rifle is even more noticeable. Fortunately wrapping your rifle in white electrician's tape will significantly disrupt its shape and outline.

1. Wrap white e-tape around handguards, buttstock, and optics while taking care to not impede the functioning of the rifle and the optics.
2. Attach twelve-inch strips of frayed e-tape in clusters with rubber bands to provide additional camouflage.

No. 005: Rifle Camouflage

CONOP: Break up the pattern of your rifle and optics in order to trick the eye of the enemy.

COA1: Rural Environment

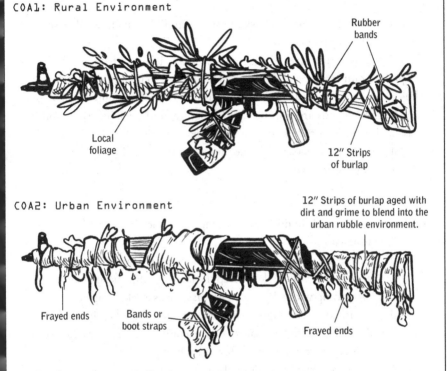

Rubber bands

Local foliage

12" Strips of burlap

COA2: Urban Environment

12" Strips of burlap aged with dirt and grime to blend into the urban rubble environment.

Frayed ends

Bands or boot straps

Frayed ends

COA3: Snow Covered Environment

Make sure scope is still operational

White electrical tape

Disrupt weapon profile

BLUF: Without effective camouflage you become the prey.

For informational purposes only,
exercise caution, prioritize safety, and obey all laws.

LATEX SCAR CONCEALMENT

Citizen soldiers are always at risk of capture and must include self-rescue preparations as part of their EDC.

There is a near-universal reluctance of most captors to frisk, pat down, or probe wounds of a detainee's intimate body parts (either male or female). For citizen soldiers, this hesitancy creates an exploitable opportunity to conceal escape aids around the vagina, rectum, and virtually every body cavity, including nostrils, ears, mouth, navel, and penis (urethra and foreskin). Rectal suppositories and tampons are ideal for concealment, but making your own latex scars provides additional opportunities. Here's how:

1. You'll need liquid latex, cooking oil, some tinfoil, and medical adhesive.
2. Coat a small piece of tinfoil and lay out a small compass, razor blade, and handcuff key. Keep the layout as thin as possible. Coat everything with a light coat of Vaseline as a release agent.
3. Begin adding a single coat of liquid latex over the kit and let it dry. Add additional coats to create a buildup over the escape aids that taper from the center toward the edges.
4. Once you reach the desired thickness and the last coat is still tacky, roll your arm across it to add texture to the surface. You can also glue armpit or pubic hair on top for additional camouflage.

Be creative with where you deploy your new "scar." The area between the base of the scrotum and the rectum, the perineum, is ideal, as are hairy armpits and the base of a women's breasts.

No. 006: Latex Scar Concealment

CONOP: If detained, well concealed escape and evasion tools may survive a thorough search.

COA1: Layout your escape aids on tinfoil and coat with a thin coat of Petroleum Jelly.

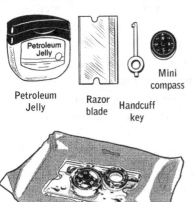

Petroleum Jelly

Razor blade

Handcuff key

Mini compass

COA2: Add coats of latex to create a buildup over the escape aids that tapers towards the edges.

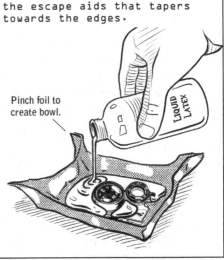

Pinch foil to create bowl.

LIQUID LATEX

COA3: Glue armpit hair or pubic hair on top for camouflage.

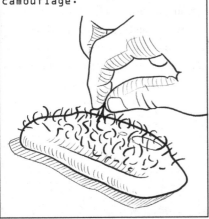

COA4: Deploy your new "scar" using medical adhesive.

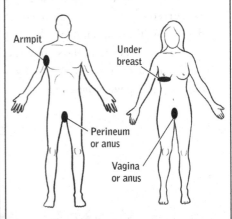

Armpit

Under breast

Perineum or anus

Vagina or anus

BLUF: Detention starts with being stripped and searched.

For informational purposes only, exercise caution, prioritize safety, and obey all laws.

TOPOGRAPHIC MAP

Reading a topographic map can be difficult if you don't understand the symbols, colors, and contour lines. However, with a little bit of practice, you can become an expert in reading and interpreting these maps. Here are some useful tips on how to read a topographic map:

First, make sure to understand the symbols and colors on the map. Symbols represent different features, such as roads, trails, buildings, and water bodies. Colors represent the different elevations on the map. Typically, green indicates lower elevations, while brown signifies higher elevations.

Next, look for the contour lines on the map. These lines connect points of the same elevation. The closer the lines are together, the steeper the terrain. If the lines are farther apart, the terrain is relatively flat.

To find the elevation of a particular location, look for the contour line that intersects the point of interest. Contour lines typically have labels indicating the elevation at that point. You can use this information to calculate the slope of the terrain.

Finally, pay attention to the direction of the contour lines. If the lines are curved or circular, it indicates a topographic feature, such as a hill or a depression. Reading a topographic map requires patience and practice. It is essential to understand the symbols, colors, and contour lines to interpret the terrain accurately. With time, you can become an expert in reading and navigating with these maps.

No. 007: Topographic Map

CONOP: Understanding the terrain requires analyzing every aspect of a topographic map.

COA1: Understand symbols of the map.

———	Road
– – – –	Path
—•—	Bridge
——+——+——	Power Line
+++++++	Railroad
☐	Building
～～	River
◯	Lake

COA2: Use Contour lines to understand the terrain elevation.

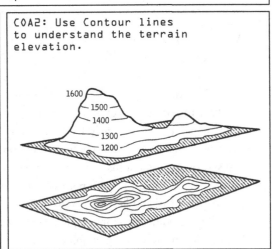

COA3: The shape and slope of the terrain can be determined by closely examining the direction and spacing of the topographic lines.

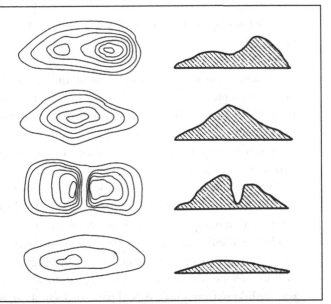

BLUF: Always identify the cliffs and peaks – and then avoid them whenever possible.

For informational purposes only,
exercise caution, prioritize safety, and obey all laws.

PLOTTING A POINT

A topographical map is a unique type of map that shows the contours and physical features of the Earth's surface. Unlike traditional maps that simply depict two-dimensional representations of features, a topographical map allows the reader to visualize the three-dimensional details of an area.

One important aspect of reading and using topographical maps is the ability to plot points accurately. Understanding how to plot points is essential because it can help you navigate through unfamiliar terrain, avoid obstacles, and stay on course. For instance, if you are hiking in a national park that is not well-marked, plotting your points can help you determine your location, distance traveled, and how far you have to go to reach your destination.

Plotting points on a topographical map also helps to identify potential hazards in an area. A topographical map can show hidden cliffs, steep inclines, and other natural features that may not be obvious to the naked eye. By plotting your points and understanding the terrain around you, you can make better decisions about how to proceed, avoid treacherous terrain, and stay safe.

Another reason why it's important to understand how to plot points on a topographical map is that it can help you plan your route ahead of time. If you are traveling through an area that you are unfamiliar with, a topographical map can help you anticipate obstacles that may lie ahead. By plotting out your course, you can see where the high points and low points are and figure out the best way to proceed.

Finally, understanding how to plot points on a topographical map is valuable because it's a critical skill for a range of outdoor activities. From hiking and camping to rock climbing and mountaineering, plotting points can help you safely and successfully navigate throughout the journey.

In conclusion, plotting points on a topographical map is an essential skill for anyone who enjoys outdoor recreation and adventure. Whether you are hiking through a national park, rock climbing at your local crag, mountaineering in a remote region, or in combat, understanding how to read and plot points on a topographical map is vital for your safety, success, and enjoyment.

No. 008: Plotting Your Location

CONOP: Accurately identifying and plotting your location on a map is essential for clear and precise navigation.

COA1: Determine the coordinates of the point.

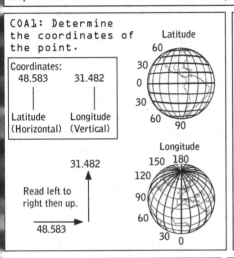

Coordinates:
48.583   31.482
| |
Latitude   Longitude
(Horizontal) (Vertical)

31.482

Read left to right then up.

48.583

COA2: Use compass or direction of sunlight to orient direction of map.

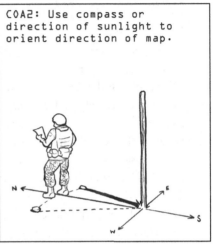

COA3: Using a straight edge, mark the lines of latitude and longitude of your location.

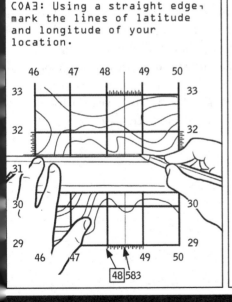

48 583

COA3: Use a pen or pencil to mark the intersection of the lines with a small dot or point.

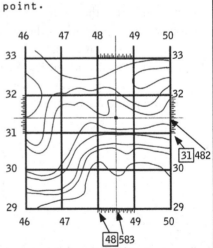

31 482

48 583

BLUF: Always triple-check your points.

NO. 009

LAND NAVIGATION

Land navigation, or orienteering, is an important skill to have for casual outdoor adventures and essential for combat. Using a map and compass to navigate through unknown terrain can ensure your safety and efficiency in reaching the destination. Firstly, it is important to have a topographical map of the area, which shows the contour lines, landmarks, and elevation levels. By studying the map, you can identify the features that will help you navigate, like water sources, hills, valleys, and road networks. Secondly, a compass is used to determine the direction and bearings to travel in. North is the key point of reference, and the compass points to magnetic north. The map is oriented to match the compass direction, and an angle is made between the map and the compass to establish the bearing to travel. The compass is then used to keep track of the direction of travel so that the person does not deviate from the path. Thirdly, it is important to track the progress on the map to ensure that the person is on the right path. This can be done by identifying landmarks, checking the distance traveled, and monitoring the location on the map. In case of any deviation, it is important to backtrack to the previous point and restart the navigation process. Lastly, it is crucial to keep updating the navigation tools as new information is obtained during the journey. Overall, land navigation using a map and compass requires some practice, but once mastered, it will enhance your outdoor skills.

No. 009: Land Navigation

CONOP: Understand how to navigate terrain with a map and compass.

COA1: Acquire a topographical map of the area.

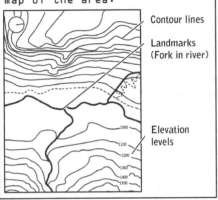

Contour lines

Landmarks (Fork in river)

Elevation levels

1000
1100
1200
1300
1400
1500

COA2: Use compass to orient direction of map.

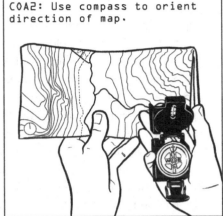

COA3: Identify landmarks and track progress with small dots.

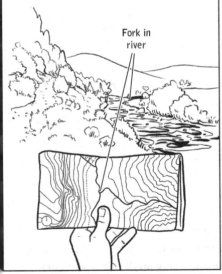

Fork in river

COA 4: Keep your map up to date by incorporating newly identified information.

Rock slide blocking route

Mark on map

BLUF: Temporarily misplacing the target does not mean that you are lost.

For informational purposes only, exercise caution, prioritize safety, and obey all laws.

GPS NAVIGATION

Special operations personnel depend on navigation skills to plot targets, determine rally points, plot personnel recovery points, and determine primary and secondary points. Citizen soldiers must be able to navigate through unfamiliar territory—often over difficult terrain and under the cover of darkness—while being tracked by hostile forces. Fortunately, the global positioning system, or GPS, now makes it possible to quickly and accurately identify your precise location and plan your route, wherever in the world you may be.

GPS systems in smartphones, handheld receivers, and even high-tech wristwatches receive signals from more than thirty satellites orbiting over 16,000 miles (26,000 kilometers) above Earth! Every GPS device is programmed to know where all the satellites are at any given time. That information—along with the amount of time the signal took to reach it—is used to figure out how far away the satellites are. By doing that, the GPS device computes its location. If your device receives signals from at least three of the many satellites, it can calculate your exact position within three meters!

GPS technology has revolutionized the way we navigate and explore the world around us. Here are some tips on how to use GPS to navigate:

1. Familiarize yourself with GPS: It's important to understand the basics of how GPS works and how to operate a GPS device. Before you hit the trail, practice with your device at home by experimenting with different settings and features.
2. Plan your route: Use GPS technology to plan your route ahead of time. You can input your desired destination and set waypoints along the way to ensure that you stay on course.
3. Calibrate your GPS: Before you start navigating, make sure your GPS is calibrated. This will help ensure that your device is accurately tracking your location and providing you with the correct information.
4. Make use of mapping software: Many GPS devices come with mapping software that allows you to download maps and satellite

No. 010: GPS Navigation

CONOP: With GPS Navigation, you can quickly determine your precise location no matter where you are.

COA 1: Connect with at least 3 satellites above you to identify your location.

COA 2: Set and save remote geo-positions to be used later for navigation.

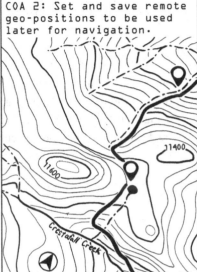

COA 4: GPS is found in most smart phones as well as handheld units and some high-tech watches.

Smartphones

GPS watch

Handheld GPS

COA 3: Enter STEALTH mode by disabling wireless connectivity and communication

BLUF: GPS is a great primary navigation tool, but always have a map and compass as a backup.

For informational purposes only,
exercise caution, prioritize safety, and obey all laws.

imagery. Use this software to familiarize yourself with the terrain and to identify potential hazards.

5. Use your GPS in addition to a map and compass: GPS technology is incredibly useful, but it's important to keep a map and compass handy, just in case. If your GPS device runs out of power or loses signals from any of the three necessary satellites, a map and compass can help you navigate your way out of a tricky situation.

GPS technology is a fantastic tool for navigating through the great outdoors. By familiarizing yourself with GPS technology, planning your route ahead of time, calibrating your GPS, using mapping software, and using your GPS alongside a map and compass, you can stay safe, stay on track, enjoy your outdoor adventure, or accomplish your mission.

CACHE SITES

Caching is the act of storing important items in a safe place, especially during emergency situations and wartime. In today's unstable world, the importance of caching important items, such as weapons, ammunition, and survival supplies, cannot be overemphasized. Natural disasters, power outages, pandemic, and other emergencies can occur unexpectedly, leaving people stranded and without access to basic necessities. Here are some reasons why caching important items is essential:

Caching important items ensures access to basic essentials during emergencies. In case of a natural disaster or power outage, access to food, water, and shelter may be limited or nonexistent. In such situations, having a cache of important items hidden nearby can make the difference between surviving and perishing.

Caching important items can help mitigate financial burdens. Prices often soar during emergencies, and stocking up on essential supplies in advance can minimize the financial burden of having to purchase them at inflated prices.

Caching important documents is also essential. Important documents, such as financial statements, passports, and medical records, can be stored securely in a cache to protect against loss or damage during an emergency.

Caching important items can provide a sense of safety and security. Knowing that essential items are stored securely and can be accessed during emergencies can provide peace of mind. This is particularly important for individuals who live in areas prone to natural disasters.

Site Selection Criteria

1. Can the site be located by simple instructions that are unmistakably clear to someone who has never visited the location? The site must have at least one distinct, permanent landmark within a readily measurable distance.
2. There should be two secure routes to and from the site, plus an escape route. All routes should provide natural concealment for private site visits. An alternate escape route may also be needed for an emergency.

No.011: Cache Sites

CONOP: Caching is often necessary to provide the secure storage of operational equipment for future use.

COA 1: Perform a site survey to identify possible locations offering privacy and access.

COA 2: Use permanent landmarks as reference points.

COA 3: Identify two safe routes to and from the site, plus an emergency escape route.

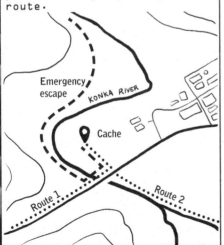

COA 4: Gather the necessary materials and prepare to fill the cache.

BLUF: Keep the location discrete and memorable. NEVER mark the map with an "X".

For informational purposes only,
exercise caution, prioritize safety, and obey all laws.

3. Can the cache be emplaced and recovered at the chosen site in all seasons? Snow on the ground is a hazard because it may make the site inaccessible and it is impossible to erase a trail in the snow.

In today's unpredictable world, caching important items has become a necessity. It ensures access to basic essentials, mitigates financial burdens, protects important documents, and provides peace of mind during emergencies. Therefore, individuals should consider caching important items as a crucial aspect of their emergency preparedness plan.

BUGOUT ROUTES

A bugout route is a preplanned escape route that you can use to quickly and safely evacuate from a dangerous or life-threatening situation. Here is a basic outline for planning bugout routes:

1. Identify potential threats: Consider the types of disasters or emergencies that are most likely to occur in your area, such as natural disasters, civil unrest, or pandemics.
2. Assess your resources: Consider what resources you have available, such as a vehicle, food and water supplies, and any medical equipment you may need.
3. Determine your destination: Decide on a safe and secure destination that you can reach quickly and easily, such as a family member's home, a designated emergency shelter, or a remote cabin.
4. Map out multiple routes: Plan several alternative routes to your destination, taking into account traffic patterns, road conditions, and potential hazards.
5. Rehearse the routes: Practice driving or walking the routes to ensure that you are familiar with the terrain and that you can reach your destination in a timely and efficient manner.
6. Update and review the routes regularly: Regularly review and update your bugout routes to ensure that they remain current and effective, taking into account any changes in the terrain or road conditions.
7. Communicate with family and friends: Ensure that your family and close friends are aware of your bugout plans and that they know the routes and destinations you have planned.

This is a basic outline, and the specific steps involved in planning bugout routes may vary depending on the types of threats, resources, and destinations you have in mind. It's important to take the time to carefully plan and prepare your bugout routes to ensure that you are prepared for any potential emergencies.

No. 012: Bugout Routes

CONOP: When disaster strikes, staying put amidst a desperate crowd fighting for the limited resources is a bad idea.

COA1:Primary Route
(Most Populated)

COA2:Alternative Route
(Back roads)

COA3:Contingency Route
(Farm Roads)

COA4:Escape Route
(Offroad)

BLUF: Bugging out is often the safest option during a crisis.

TWO-WAY RADIO COMMUNICATIONS

"Zero tech" is always the safest (see skill no. 041) type of communication, but there are times where your squad may not all be within in line of sight (LOS) and a radio/frequency signal is required. Though "black phones" are handy (see skill no. 015), they may not always be available.

In such instances, MURS (Multi-Use Radio Service) radios are license-free, relatively low-cost, two-way communication systems for use over short distances: two to eight miles. While their range is limited, low-power radio signals are more desirable and more difficult for the enemy to intercept and track.

Since MURS communications are not encrypted, citizens can use brevity codes to convey complex information with only a few words or codes. Typically, each team member carries a laminated waterproof card listing their predetermined brevity codes.

In a similar manner, a predetermined number of radio clicks can also be used to convey information, such as two clicks may mean that the sniper is in position and four clicks may mean that the target is entering the kill zone.

Every fire team mission should also be assigned an operational number just before the mission begins for recognition or signal verification. For example, if the operational number is thirteen, you can challenge with any other number, such as four, and the response nine must add up to.

Discretion is important for covert radio use, and earpieces and a small throat microphone will help conceal its existence. Be sure to cover the display screen on the radio with black tape to block the compromising glow it gives off.

No. 013: Two-Way Radio Communication

CONOP: Low-power two-way radios are harder to track and provide reliable communications when "black phones" are unavailable.

COA1: Examples of brevity code words

Brevity Code Word	Meaning
Bent	System is Broken
Bogey	Group with unknown identity
Push	Switch to designated frequency
Status	Request for an individual's tactical situation
Visual	Spotting of friendly position

COA2: Examples of click-codes.

Click Codes	Meaning
1	Yes
2	No
3	Target in Sight
4	Challenge call
5	Bump
6	Abort
7+	Help

COA3: Use earpieces and concealed microphones to mask radio use and keep hands free.

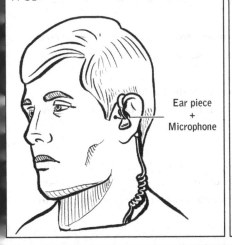

Ear piece
+
Microphone

COA4: Use black tape to mask the glow given off by the display screen.

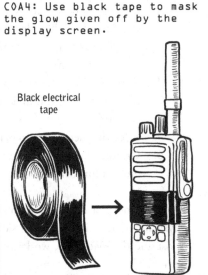

Black electrical tape

BLUF: Two-way radios may be necessary for citizens to operate efficiently.

For informational purposes only,
exercise caution, prioritize safety, and obey all laws.

FARADAY BOX

"Going dark" to block all incoming and outgoing signals to your mobile phone will protect against tracking, targeting, hackers, and eavesdroppers. A Faraday box, or Faraday cage, allows you to block all incoming and outgoing EMF signals, including 4G, 5G, Wi-Fi, Bluetooth, and GPS, to help isolate and protect your cell phones, tablets, and other electronics from remote eavesdropping, hacking, location tracking, and EMP damage.

Faraday cages can be small and portable or large enough to hold multiple mobile devices. For soldiers, an effective Faraday cage can be improvised inexpensively on the battlefield.

Scrounge a metal ammo can that is large enough to hold the mobile electronic device(s) to be protected.

1. Remove the rubber gasket on the lid and wrap it tinfoil.
2. Use a grinder to remove the paint and expose bare metal where the lid seals against the can.
3. Cut pieces of cardboard to line the inside of the top, bottom, and walls of the can.
4. Turn off and place each of the electronic devices to be protected securely inside an individual plastic bag and lay them on top of the cardboard base.
5. Place the metal lid into place to create a secure seal.
6. Ground the box with a wire running to a metal tent pole in the ground for further protection.

Warning: If any part of a mobile device is allowed to touch or make physical contact with the metal sides of the Faraday cage, all protection is lost and the metal cage works as an antenna that can make it easier to be tracked!

No. 014: Faraday Box

CONOP: A faraday box blocks all signals emitted by mobile phone and electronics.

COA1: Remove the rubber gasket on the ammunition box lid and wrap it in tin-foil.

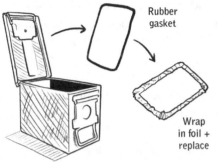

Rubber gasket

Wrap in foil + replace

COA:2 Remove paint and expose bare metal where the lid seals against the can. Replace foil covered rubber gasket.

COA3: Cut pieces of cardboard to line the inside of the top, bottom, and walls of the can.

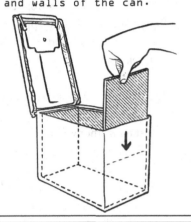

COA4: Place each of the electronic devices to be protected securely inside a plastic sandwich bag and lay them on top of the cardboard base.

COA5: Clamp the metal lid and gasket into place to create a secure seal.

Metal tent pole

COA6: Ground the box with a wire running to a metal tent pole in the ground for further attenuation.

BLUF: "Go dark" or become a target.

OPERATIONAL PHONE

"Black" (covert) operational flip phones are essential for fire team missions to evade enemy eavesdroppers and tracking. Since older, basic-feature flip phones don't have apps or access the internet, they are immune to traditional viruses and there's no way for hackers to get into your device or track you.

1. Anonymity: If someone does not want to reveal their identity to others or is concerned about privacy, a black phone can be a useful tool for staying anonymous.
2. Safety: Black phones are less expensive than regular phones and can serve as a backup phone for emergencies or travel. They are easy to replace if lost or stolen, and they cannot be tracked to the owner.
3. Security: Black phones can be used to increase security because they are difficult to trace. This feature is useful for journalists, activists, and people who work in high-risk professions.
4. Cost-effectiveness: Black phones are typically cheaper than regular mobile phones and can often be purchased without a contract or monthly fees.
5. Short-term use: Since these phones are disposable, they can be used for specific periods, such as while traveling or for a short-term project, and discarded afterward.

Here is how to create an operational set of "black" phones for your fire team:

1. Beg, borrow, buy, confiscate, or steal older, basic-feature (non-internet) flip phones for each member of your pack. Preowned phones should be obtained anonymously and are preferred for greater security.
2. Make certain that the phones will operate on the frequencies used by your local cell providers, and protect each of your phones with a secure password or PIN.

No.015: Operational Phone

CONOP: Use dumb flip phones that don't have apps or internet access to prevent viruses, hacking, and tracking.

COA1: Beg, borrow, buy, confiscate, or steal older basic-feature (non-internet) flip-phones.

Beg

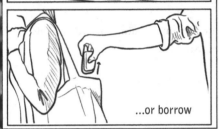

...or borrow

COA2: Activate the flip phones in a remote area away from your base and make a call.

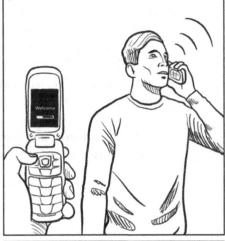

Welcome

COA3: Hang up during the call, remove flip-phone batteries, and store all "Black" phones in a farady box.

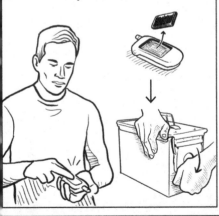

COA4: Distribute "Black" phones just before an operation and activate them when you are away from your base.

BLUF: Reverting to a flip-phone can save your life.

For informational purposes only,
exercise caution, prioritize safety, and obey all laws.

3. Take all phones to a remote area miles away from your base or AOR (area of operations) and activate each flip phone to make a call. While your phone is connected on the call, simply hang up and remove the battery from the phone. Doing so will cause the phone to remain logged into the remote cell tower.
4. Store all "black" phones (without batteries) inside a Faraday cage (see skill no. 014) until needed.
5. Before an operation, travel from your base to a neutral location away from your base or operational area before replacing batteries and activating the flip phones.
6. Distribute the flip phones to team members for the mission.
7. After the operation, repeat step no. 3 (above) before deactivating the flip phones and placing them back inside the Faraday cage.

Note: If the old-style flip phones are unavailable, anonymously purchase inexpensive burner phones and SIM cards and pay with cash.

EMERGENCY MEDICAL KIT

Medical kits aren't sexy and are often overlooked. However, in wartime 90 percent of combat fatalities occur prior to arrival at a medical facility. A full 25 percent of those fatalities might have survived if self-aid and buddy-aid occurred soon after the injury.

Care under fire: Care rendered at the scene of the injury. Available medical equipment in combat is often limited to the supplies carried by each citizen soldier. This stage focuses on a quick assessment and placing a tourniquet on any major bleed.

Tactical field dare: Rendered once clear of hostile fire. The treatment rendered varies depending on the skill level of the provider and medical supplies available. Time prior to evacuation may range from a few minutes to many hours. Care here may include advanced airway treatment, IV therapy, etc.

Your personal medical kit should be carried in a small bag and include the following:

- EpiPen for your allergies
- two tourniquets (we recommend CAT7 TQ and SAM XT OR)
- two sets emergency trauma dressing—six inches flat
- two vented chest seals (we recommend a two-pack of Hyfins)
- two triangle bandages
- one roll of surgical tape
- twenty flexible fabric bandages
- twelve tubes of antibiotic ointment
- twenty antiseptic towelettes
- two nasopharyngeal airway kits
- one roll of combat gauze with hemostatic bandage
- two packs NAR wound-packing gauze
- one polycarbonate eye shield
- trauma shears

No. 016: Emergency Medical Kit

CONOP: Be prepared for emergency medical care for yourself or a buddy at all times.

COA 1: Gather the medical supplies and a small bag.

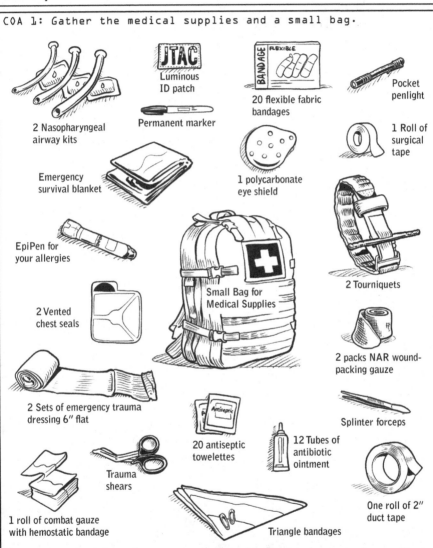

2 Nasopharyngeal airway kits

JTAC Luminous ID patch

Permanent marker

20 flexible fabric bandages

Pocket penlight

Emergency survival blanket

1 polycarbonate eye shield

1 Roll of surgical tape

EpiPen for your allergies

Small Bag for Medical Supplies

2 Tourniquets

2 Vented chest seals

2 packs NAR wound-packing gauze

2 Sets of emergency trauma dressing 6" flat

20 antiseptic towelettes

12 Tubes of antibiotic ointment

Splinter forceps

Trauma shears

1 roll of combat gauze with hemostatic bandage

Triangle bandages

One roll of 2" duct tape

- splinter forceps
- emergency survival blanket
- permanent marker
- pocket penlight with working batteries
- luminous ID patch
- one roll of two-inch duct tape

EMERGENCY TOURNIQUET

Creating and applying a tourniquet is a relatively simple technique that can help control blood loss following a traumatic injury. Used for wounds occurring on the limbs, the device compresses the area around the injury to limit blood flow until the wound can be treated and closed.

Tourniquets should be applied immediately if bleeding cannot be stopped using direct pressure alone. Heavy and uncontrolled bleeding can cause death within minutes, so it's necessary to act quickly.

Tourniquets can be improvised with almost anything that uses circumferential pressure. Many improvised materials can be effective, such as belts (see skill no. 032), shirt sleeves, pant legs, scarves, bandanas, and even the charging cable on your mobile phone. Ideally a tourniquet should be two to four inches wide to evenly distribute the pressure around the limb. Professional tourniquets are preferred, but alternatives will work in an emergency.

What used to be last option is now the first option. The new rule for tourniquet (T) placement is simple. "Go high or die." Always put the T as high up the limb as possible, regardless of where the bleeding occurs. If you have enough material, wrap it a few times to create padding. When using fabric, twist a short stick or other rigid object, like a pen, on the outside layer of the tourniquet to create a torsion device to stop blood loss.

A tourniquet should only be used in an emergency until you're able to receive additional medical attention. After two hours, neurovascular injury can occur.

No.017: Emergency Tourniquet

CONOP: Heavy and uncontrolled bleeding can cause death within minutes, so act quickly.

COA 1: Expose the wound by removing any clothing or gear.

COA 2: Apply constant pressure on the wound with gauze or strips of cloth.

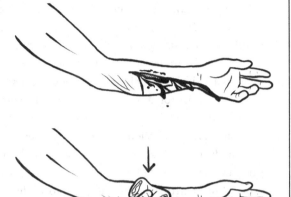

COA 3: Improvise a tourniquet as high on the limb as possible, but never on a joint or the neck or torso.

Power cord

Metal pen

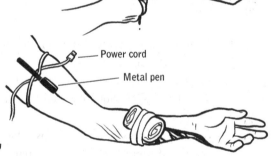

COA 4: Create a torsion device to slow bleeding and tie in place when it stops. Get to a doctor as soon as possible.

Wrap power cord around pen and twist tight.

Secure pen in place with remaining length of cord.

BLUF: Go high or die.

COMBAT ROLL

Rescuing a wounded teammate is a solemn responsibility. No one is ever left behind. The task, however, is especially difficult if he is badly injured or unconscious and you must run one hundred yards with him on your shoulder while under hostile fire. Dead lifting two hundred pounds or more (with kit) is nearly impossible, but fortunately there is another way.

The combat roll is a series of fluid movements that can be performed from a standing, kneeling, or lying position to enable you to hoist a fallen teammate onto your shoulder and into a fireman's carry within a couple of seconds. From that position, you can carry him for about one hundred yards before muscle fatigue sets in. It minimizes the time that you are exposed while lifting and moving him to a safer position.

Move as follows from a standing position with your teammate lying on his back.

1. Approach from his feet and grab his right pants leg above the ankle with your left hand.
2. Lift his right leg as you reach beneath his right thigh with your other hand. Grab hold of his uniform as you do a roll across his chest.
3. Roll to your knees with your hips below his shoulders.
4. Stand and adjust his body into a fireman's carry.
5. Retrieve his weapon and equipment with your free hand and begin moving. Don't leave anything behind.

No. 018: Combat Roll

CONOP: Employing a combat roll allows an operator to lift a fallen buddy and carry him to safety.

Make sure the victim is flat on their back.

COA1: Approach victim and grab their right leg with your left hand.

COA2: Lift their right leg while dropping your right shoulder.

COA3: Roll over your right shoulder while pulling his leg with your momentum.

Collect arm

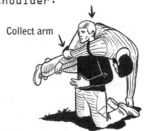

COA4: Complete the roll on your knees with the victim directly above your hips.

COA5: Come to one knee.

COA6: Stand with the victim's weight centered.

BLUF: No one is ever left behind.

For informational purposes only, exercise caution, prioritize safety, and obey all laws.

KNIFE QUICK DRAW

As a citizen soldier, you should ideally carry your concealed pistol and a concealed fixed blade knife. You're probably asking yourself why you would need both when a pistol can resolve most problems. The difference is proximity and/or entanglement with your adversary, especially if you get caught off guard. Under certain circumstances it is exponentially faster to draw a fixed blade knife and deliver a lethal strike than drawing a pistol and pulling the trigger.

First and foremost, you want to carry and conceal a fixed blade instead of a folding knife, which requires extra steps to be deployed. A fixed blade knife can be easily concealed inside pants at the appendix or twelve o'clock position or on your hip at the three o'clock position if you're right-handed.

Drawing your fixed blade knife will take practice, but you will find that in a short period of time you'll become faster and more efficient. Use two hands in the movement. The fingers of your support hand (the hand not drawing the blade) rake the shirt and other layers of clothing up and away from the body to expose the knife handle. Simultaneously the knife hand acquires a confident grip and completes the draw.

The goal is to drive the tip of the knife from the holster directly to your adversary's face. Don't stop with the initial blow. Continue moving, flanking and stabbing your adversary until you can escape safely.

No. 019: Knife Quick Draw

CONOP: A quick draw technique is essential for swiftly retrieving a concealed knife when seconds count.

COA1: Acquire a fixed blade and sheath.

COA2: Clip knife inside pants at 12:00 or 3:00 position.

3:00   12:00

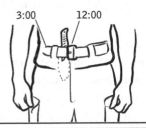

Avoid Folding Knives

A

B

COA 3:Quick Draw:

A. Keep hands in front to maintain distance from attacker.

B. Use left hand to rake shirt upwards.

C. Grab knife handle.

D. Thrust upwards towards the attacker's face.

C

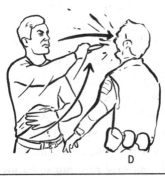

D

Reverse Grip

Blade edge

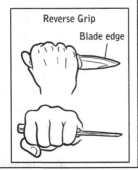

BLUF: Prepare for the unexpected: learn the knife quick draw.

For informational purposes only,
exercise caution, prioritize safety, and obey all laws.

NO. 020

WEAPONS SAFETY

Gun safety is paramount at all times because firearms are deadly weapons that can cause irreparable harm to human life and property. Even the slightest negligence or carelessness can lead to fatal accidents that have far-reaching consequences. Proper handling, usage, and storage of firearms are essential to prevent unintended discharge, theft, or misuse. Gun safety education and awareness are crucial to reducing the risks associated with firearms. It is important to remember that guns do not discriminate and that everyone, including children, should be taught the importance of gun safety to ensure responsible ownership and prevent accidental shootings.

The five rules of weapons safety rules are as important in wartime as they are in peacetime.

1. Treat every weapon as if it is loaded. A rifle is a tool for killing the enemy. The first rule of weapons safety ensures that the rifle and every firearm are treated with the appropriate respect. A weapon is never safe to handle until you have cleared it.
2. Keep your finger straight and off the trigger until you intend to fire. This rule is another way to ensure that while handling your weapon, you do not unintentionally pull the trigger while on patrol or moving in and out of vehicles or tight spaces.
3. Never point your weapon at anything you don't intend to kill. This rule means keeping the muzzle of your rifle always pointed in a safe direction, regardless of whether it is loaded or not.
4. Keep your weapon on safe until you intend to fire. All weapons are equipped with a mechanical safety.
5. Know your target and what is beyond it. This means that you have positive identification that the target is a threat, and you are cleared to legally engage them. Once you have positive identification, you may run into scenarios where it is still not safe to shoot. Bullets go through people and walls so you need to be as confident as possible that you can engage the threat without harming innocent people caught in the gunfire.

No. 020: Weapons Safety

CONOP: Treat every weapon as if it is loaded.

COA1: Know your weapons'
safety features or lack
of...

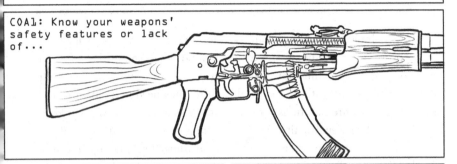

COA2: Keep your finger off the
trigger until you intend to
fire.

COA3: Never point your weapon
at anything you don't intend
to kill.

COA4: Keep your weapon on
safe until you intend to
fire.

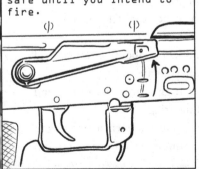

COA5: Know your target and
what is beyond it.

BLUF: Don't point your weapon at anything you don't want to kill.

NO. 021

EXPERT RIFLE

Target shooting is an important skill for a soldier because it helps them improve their accuracy, speed, and overall marksmanship. Effective shooting is a fundamental requirement for combat, and target shooting provides soldiers with the essential training they need to handle firearms in high-pressure situations. Practicing target shooting also helps soldiers develop their visual acuity, focus, and attention to detail. These skills are crucial to remaining calm and composed under fire, making informed decisions, and executing tasks precisely. Target shooting also helps soldiers improve their confidence and mental toughness under stressful conditions and makes them better equipped to handle combat situations. In conclusion, target shooting is a valuable activity that plays a vital role in shaping the skills and capabilities of a soldier, making them more effective and reliable on the battlefield.

The proper technique for shooting a rifle accurately includes the following steps:

1. Stance: Stand with your feet shoulder-width apart and a slight bend in your knees for stability.
2. Grip: Hold the rifle firmly with your nonfiring hand and wrap your firing hand around the pistol grip.
3. Sight alignment: Line up the front and rear sights so they are vertically aligned and centered on the target.
4. Breathing: Take a deep breath and let out about half, then hold your breath for a moment to steady your aim.
5. Trigger control: Slowly squeeze the trigger with your firing hand until it breaks. Don't pull or jerk the trigger.
6. Follow-through: Keep the rifle steady for a moment after firing to ensure proper follow-through and minimize the impact of recoil.

It's important to practice these techniques regularly to develop good muscle memory and shooting habits. Additionally, seeking professional instruction can help refine and improve your shooting technique.

No. 021: Expert Rifle

CONOP: Rifles are the most important weapons on the battlefield.

COA1: Stand with your feet shoulder-width apart and knees slightly bent.

COA2: Grip: Hold the rifle firmly with your non-firing hand and wrap your firing hand around the pistol grip.

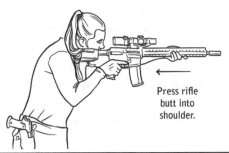

Press rifle butt into shoulder.

COA3: Sight alignment: Line up cross hairs so they are centered on the target.

COA4: Breathing: Take a deep breath and let out about half, then hold your breath for a moment to steady your aim.

COA5: Trigger control: Slowly squeeze the trigger with your firing hand until it breaks. Don't pull or jerk the trigger.

COA6: Follow-through: Keep the rifle steady and ready for the next engagement.

BLUF: Long rifles are the true source of power on the battlefield.

For informational purposes only,
exercise caution, prioritize safety, and obey all laws.

NO. 022

ZERO A RIFLE

Zeroing, or sighting in, is the process of aligning your firearm's sights or scope with the point of impact on your target. Zeroing is an important step that shooters should take before using their firearm for any purpose, whether it is hunting, target shooting, or self-defense.

Zeroing ensures that your firearm is shooting accurately, which is crucial for making ethical shots when hunting and avoiding unintended casualties during combat. Rifles are more dangerous if they are not accurately zeroed in. It is also an important safety measure as it eliminates guesswork and prevents accidental shootings.

In a self-defense situation, accuracy is essential. If a firearm is not zeroed, the shooter may miss the intended target and hit an innocent bystander. Additionally, zeroing your rifle at the range ensures you know where to aim at the target in order to hit the bull's-eye.

Overall, zeroing is an important step in ensuring that your firearm is accurate and shoots precisely, both for your safety and for the ethical practice of hunting. It is important for anyone who uses a firearm with an optical sight to take time to practice and zero the scope so they can hit their target accurately.

Sighting in a rifle is the process of adjusting the iron sights or optics on the rifle so that the bullet will hit the target at the desired point of impact. Here is a general process for sighting in a rifle:

1. Set up a target at a known distance, typically one hundred yards for most rifles. Personally, I like to start at twenty-five yards and ensure I actually hit the target and then work my way back to one hundred yards.
2. Set up a stable shooting position, using a rest, sandbags, or a full ruck or backpack.
3. Fire a few shots (three to five, depending on how much money you have) to get a rough zero, or starting point, for your adjustments.
4. Using a spotting scope or binoculars, observe where the bullets are hitting in relation to your target.

No. 022: How to Zero a Rifle

CONOP: Zeroing in a rifle's optics can greatly improve a shooter's accuracy.

COA1: Set up target at 25 yards and establish a stable firing position.

25 Yards

COA2: Fire a few shots aimed at the center of the target.

Shot grouping to left and down of center.

COA 3: Make adjustments to windage and elevation based on where the bullets are hitting.

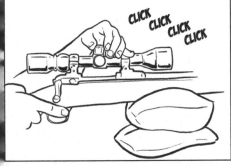

CLICK CLICK CLICK CLICK

COA 4: Fire a few more shots and check your adjustments. Repeat steps 2 and 3 until your shots are hitting the desired point of impact.

COA 5: Move to 50 and 100 yards and repeat the process.

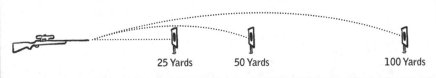

25 Yards   50 Yards   100 Yards

BLUF: Your rifle is only as accurate as its zero'd.

5. Make adjustments to the iron sights or optics based on where the bullets are hitting. For example, if the bullets are hitting to the left of the target, adjust the windage knob (left and right adjustment) to the right. If the bullets are hitting too high, adjust the elevation knob (up and down adjustment) to lower the point of impact.

6. Fire a few more shots and check your adjustments. Repeat steps 4 and 5 until your shots are hitting the desired point of impact.

7. Once you are satisfied with your adjustments, fire several more shots to confirm your new zero.

It's important to note that the above process is a general guideline, and the specific steps and equipment may vary depending on the type of rifle, sight or optic being used. Additionally, different types of shooting may require different zero distance, for example for long-range shooting, zeroing at two hundred or three hundred yards may be needed.

SINGLE-POINT TACTICAL SLING

Single-point tactical slings have gained in popularity because of their use by special operations personnel. The design isn't new, however, and originated during the America Civil War to sling cavalry carbines. The single-point design permits the citizen to transition firing from either shoulder or drop the weapon and let it hang downward while still attached to their body. This sling design allows the citizen's hands to remain free when the rifle is not needed and is more comfortable for patrolling. The sling's loop design around the neck and shoulder lightens your load, making patrolling with a weapon less strenuous.

You can purchase a single-point tactical sling online or make one yourself for only a few dollars using web straps (or lashing straps). You'll need the following:

- sixty inches of 1.5-inch, thin, nylon webbing
- twelve inches of one-inch webbing (or a size to fit your sling swivel)
- one one-inch slide
- one 1.5-inch buckle
- four 1.5-inch slides
- scissors and a lighter to burn the frayed edges

You'll be crafting two components: the base and the sling. The base remains attached to the weapon and connects with a buckle to the neck/shoulder sling.

- To create the base, mount the one-inch slide on the one-inch nylon webbing and place it through your sling swivel, just above the rifle's center of gravity.
- Create the sling with the loop that goes around your neck and shoulder.
- Connect the two sections and adjust the sling's length so that the rifle hangs freely (pointed down) and adjust the length for comfort and maneuverability.

No. 023: How to Make a Single-Point Tactical Sling

CONOP: A single-point tactical sling frees the operator's hands while keeping the weapon within easy reach.

COA1: Acquire webbing, thread and needle, scissors, a carabiner, and a lighter.

COA2: Cut a large piece of the webbing that goes around your neck and shoulder. The smaller piece connects to the rifle.

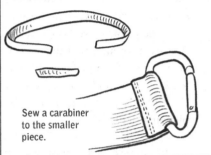

Sew a carabiner to the smaller piece.

COA3: Use a fisher's knot to complete the big loop leaving enough material to tie another fisher's knot to the small strip.

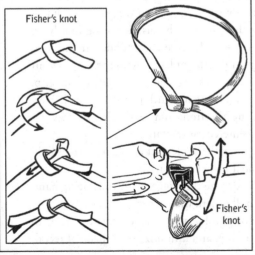

Fisher's knot

Fisher's knot

COA4: Adjust the length for comfort and maneuverability.

Burn ends to keep the webbing from unraveling.

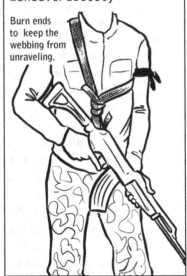

BLUF: Lessen your load and avoid unnecessary strain by using a single-point sling.

For informational purposes only, exercise caution, prioritize safety, and obey all laws.

EXPERT PISTOL

Having a secondary weapon like a pistol is crucial for soldiers operating in a combat zone. It provides them with a backup plan in case their primary weapon malfunctions or runs out of ammunition. The pistol also provides a portable and convenient weapon option for close-range engagements when the primary weapon is not practical. It may also allow soldiers to carry extra ammunition that is compatible with both weapons. Overall, a secondary weapon like a pistol can provide soldiers with an extra layer of defense and an added advantage on the battlefield.

The proper technique for shooting a pistol accurately includes the following steps:

1. Stance: Stand with your feet shoulder-width apart and a slight bend in your knees for stability.
2. Grip: Ensure your dominant hand is positioned high on the backstrap of the pistol grip, with the webbing between your thumb and index finger pressed firmly against the tang of the grip. Wrap your fingers around the grip. Your trigger finger should be extended alongside the frame of the pistol, resting lightly on the outside of the trigger guard. Place your nondominant hand around the fingers of your dominant hand, with the base of your nondominant thumb snugly resting against the side of the grip. Both thumbs should be pointing forward, parallel to the barrel.
3. Sight alignment: Line up the front and rear sights so they are vertically aligned and centered on the target.
4. Breathing: Take a deep breath and let out about half, then hold your breath for a moment to steady your aim.
5. Trigger control: Slowly squeeze the trigger with your firing hand until it breaks. Don't pull or jerk the trigger.
6. Follow-through: Keep the pistol steady for a moment after firing to ensure proper follow-through and minimize the impact of recoil.

It's important to practice these techniques regularly to develop good muscle memory and shooting habits. Additionally, seeking professional instruction can help refine and improve your shooting technique.

No. 024: Expert Pistol

CONOP: Skill with the handgun is essential for resistance operations.

COA1: Stand with your feet shoulder-width apart and knees slightly bent.

Feet shoulder width apart.

COA2: Grip

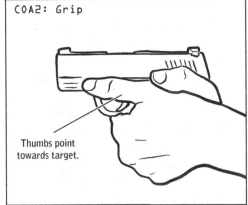

Thumbs point towards target.

COA3: Sight alignment: Line up the front and rear sights so they are horizontally aligned and centered on the target.

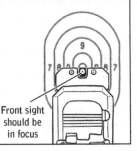

Front sight should be in focus

COA4: Breathing: Take a deep breath and let out about half, then hold your breath for a moment to steady your aim.

COA5: Trigger control: Slowly squeeze the trigger with your firing hand until it breaks. Don't pull or jerk the trigger.

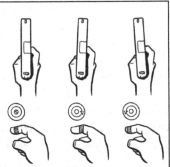

COA6: Follow-through: Keep the pistol steady and ready for the next engagement.

BLUF: A pistol is always secondary to a rifle.

NO. 025

IMPROVISED NIGHT SIGHTS

Night sights on a rifle or pistol are a good idea because they allow the shooter to aim and shoot accurately in low light conditions or complete darkness. These sights emit a small amount of light, which illuminates the sight picture making it easily visible. This feature helps shooters to quickly acquire the target and accurately engage it. It increases overall accuracy and reduces the likelihood of missing the target. Night sights are also useful for home defense purposes, where low light conditions are common and quick access to a firearm may be necessary. In short, night sights on a rifle or pistol provide an added layer of safety, accuracy, and convenience for shooters.

Low-light shooting accuracy can be enhanced using night vision goggles (NVGs) or with luminescent gun sights. Many pistols come with tritium (luminescent) sites but dim with age or wear off over time. Fluorescent gun site paint may be reapplied, but if supplies are unavailable, you can make your own improvised luminescing gun sites with glowing fishing lures!

Glowing worms and similar lures mix phosphorescent powders into the rubber before the lures are molded. Pigment particles in the powder are charged (excited) by most any visible light or instantaneously by ultraviolet light. Photoluminescent pigment releases energy in the form of visible light (glowing in the dark) for as long as twenty-four hours, depending on the color. Green is the preferred color for gun sites.

Glowing fishing lures can be carefully cut into tiny bits with a sharp knife or razor blade, repurposed, and glued onto existing gun sites that have dimmed or worn off. Here's how:

1. Carefully scrape away any existing paint and clean the metal with alcohol.
2. Mix the tiny bits of the fishing lures with a small amount of clear silicon glue and place into position with a small brush or toothpick. Allow to dry and cure for seventy-two hours before holstering.

Improvised suppressors (see skill no. 078) eliminate the usefulness of existing pistol sights. However, you can create an aiming stripe on the back of the filter using the technique above. Add marks at the three and nine o'clock positions for even better accuracy.

No. 025: Make Improvised Night Sights

CONOP: Luminescing gun sights increase shooting accuracy in low-light conditions.

COA1: Acquire a supply of glowing fishing lures and cut into tiny bits with a razor blade.

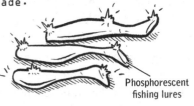

Phosphorescent fishing lures

Finely chopped

COA2: Scrape the existing sights and clean with alcohol.

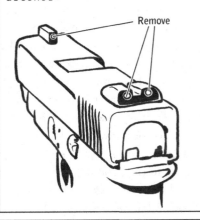

Remove

COA3: Mix the glowing bits with clear silicon glue and paint onto the gun sight.

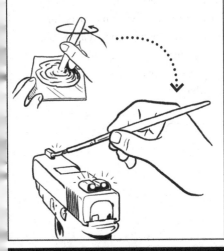

COA4: Add a vertical aiming stripe and two reference marks (at 3 & 9 o'clock) on the back of an oil filter suppressor for greater accuracy.

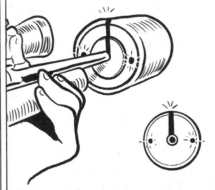

BLUF: Give your night sights a good dose of sunlight before moonlight.

NO. 026

SLICE THE PIE

Slicing the "pie" is an essential tactic for close quarters combat (CQC). It can be applied by anyone facing obstacles that may conceal unknown threats, such as rooms, doors, closets, hallways, vehicles, corners of buildings, and even open areas. Learning to properly slice the pie will allow you to utilize maximum cover/concealment before overcommitting.

The fundamental way to employ the tactic is when approaching a doorway to a room that may conceal a threat(s). You should be looking to identify a person, or any part of one, as well as IEDs and other threats.

As you draw close, allow enough room to fully extended your weapon. A common mistake when learning this tactic is to position yourself too close to the door and make yourself a more prominent target. Stepping back a couple of steps, however, may allow you to use other available cover and still be able to engage the adversary before he can engage you.

Identify the axis around which you can rotate to examine as much of the room as possible, one slice at a time. Move slowly and methodically around the apex of the curve in small side steps. Don't move faster than you can effectively engage any threat that appears. As you move, take advantage of any available cover. Maintain your posture and weapon at a low-ready position to allow for a full field of view into the room.

The tactic works equally well when approaching an unknown vehicle or clearing a room in your home for intruders.

No. 026: Slicing the Pie

CONOP: Clearing rooms, vehicles, and other obstacles to identify threats is an essential skill.

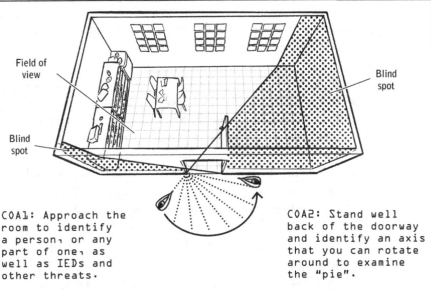

Field of view

Blind spot

Blind spot

COA1: Approach the room to identify a person, or any part of one, as well as IEDs and other threats.

COA2: Stand well back of the doorway and identify an axis that you can rotate around to examine the "pie".

COA3: Maintain your posture and weapon at a high ready position.

COA4: Using small side steps move around the curve at a speed that allows to engage any threat that appears in your field of view.

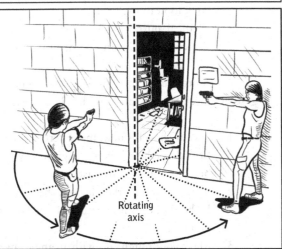

Rotating axis

BLUF: Eat the pie slowly... one slice at a time.

For informational purposes only, exercise caution, prioritize safety, and obey all laws.

COMBAT SHOVEL

The combat shovel is a versatile tool that serves various purposes for the citizen soldier, including the following:

- Digging: A combat shovel can dig trenches, foxholes, and defensive positions in a combat zone.
- Camouflage: Soldiers can use the combat shovel to gather natural materials, such as dirt, leaves, and branches, to camouflage their positions.
- Breaching: The sharpened edge of a combat shovel can be used to break through locks and doors to gain entry where necessary.
- Self-defense: In the absence of a primary weapon, a combat shovel can be used as a close-combat weapon for self-defense.
- Vehicle recovery: A combat shovel can help to remove debris and obstacles to recover stuck vehicles.
- Cooking: Soldiers can use a combat shovel to dig a firepit and cook food in the field.
- Medical purposes: A combat shovel can serve as a makeshift stretcher or splint in case of a medical emergency.

An improvised combat shovel can be crafted from a small spade or garden shovel. Select a model with a flatter head to make it easier to throw.

1. If your shovel is new, make certain that the handle is sturdy and firmly attached. If you're beginning with an old shovel, use a wire brush to remove any rust.
2. With a black marker, lay out the shape of your new shovelhead. It should be approximately six inches by ten inches and slightly pointed.
3. Make your rough cuts with an angle saw and then refine the shape with a belt grinder.
4. Sharpen the blade on three sides using a grinder, polishing stone, or rough piece of concrete.

No. 027: Combat Shovel

CONOP: A combat shovel is a multi-purpose tool for digging and fighting.

COA 1: With a black marker lay out the shape of your new shovel head.

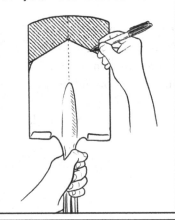

COA 2: Make your rough cuts with an angle saw and then refine the shape with a belt grinder.

COA 3: Sharpen the blade on three sides using a grinder, polishing stone, or a rough piece of concrete.

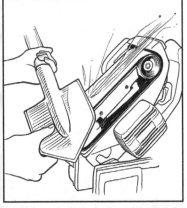

COA 4: Cut a swale into the bottom of the shaft and size to 19.6".

Pommel

19.6"

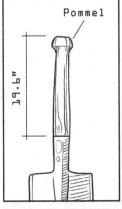

COA 5: Camouflage your shovel with paint, or use boiled linseed oil to protect the wood.

boiled linseed oil

BLUF: Your shovel should always be at your side.

For informational purposes only,
exercise caution, prioritize safety, and obey all laws.

5. Your finished blade should receive a coat of gun-blue or rust-inhibiting paint for protection.

6. The ideal length of your finished combat shovel should be fifty centimeters (19.6 inches) and weigh two pounds or less. Take care to remove any slick finishes on the handle, such as varnish, and refinish with boiled linseed oil (BLO). If needed, paint your handle in camouflage colors and spray the blade with a flat-green or flat-gray paint.

7. Use your belt grinder and cut a swale into the end of the handle to make it easier to maneuver and throw. Adding a six-inch Ranger Band above the swale will provide an even better grip, and drilling a small hole will allow you to add a paracord lanyard.

Your combat shovel is ready for digging or maneuvering as a tomahawk or battle-ax.

THE SMALL SHOVEL IN COMBAT

Your primary weapons are your short barrel rifle, your pistol as a backup, and then there's the shovel—yes, a shovel. The multipurpose entrenching spade is a highly effective weapon for close quarters combat (CQC). It can help you dig a trench, paddle a boat, as well as bludgeon, maim, slash, decapitate, stab, and bury an attacker.

WWI soldiers learned that once an enemy was in the trenches, their six-foot-long rifle bayonets were cumbersome, unwieldy, and ill-suited for the narrow confines. Their improvised solution was to sharpen the handy fifty-centimeter (19.6-inch) sapper spade on three sides to convert it into a multisided weapon.

The same sharp edges originally designed to cut through roots sliced just as easily the necks of an enemy. The modified spade was not only useful for jabbing a man under the chin, but the result of its two-pound heft was that if the enemy was struck between the neck and shoulder, it easily cleaved through the trapezius muscle, clavicle and into the chest cavity. The small tool proved more effective for cutting and thrusting at close quarters than either a bayonet or fighting knife and combined the best attributes of a battle-ax with a war club. In a pinch, it may even stop some pistol rounds!

One hundred years later, the small sapper spade still excels at digging fighting positions and can be used as a terrifying weapon that enables a single citizen to hold off multiple attackers. Afterward it becomes useful for burying the bodies and site cleanup. Even better, it's a nonalerting tool that can accompany you (in your checked luggage or the trunk of your vehicle) on any trip and can protect you in your vehicle, hotel room, or in the field.

No. 028: Use of a Shovel in Combat

CONOP: The small shovel is a versatile fighting weapon for stabbing, slashing, and throwing.

COA 1: Short Handed Shovel

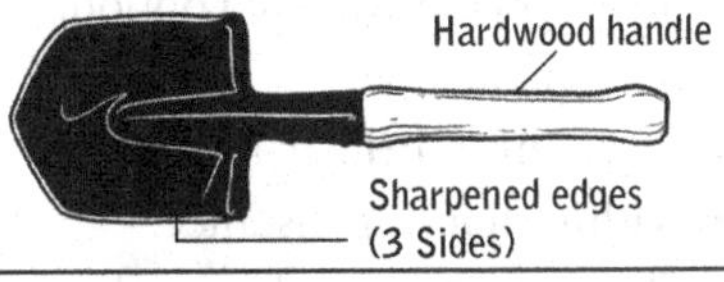
Hardwood handle
Sharpened edges
(3 Sides)

COA 2: Areas to Target

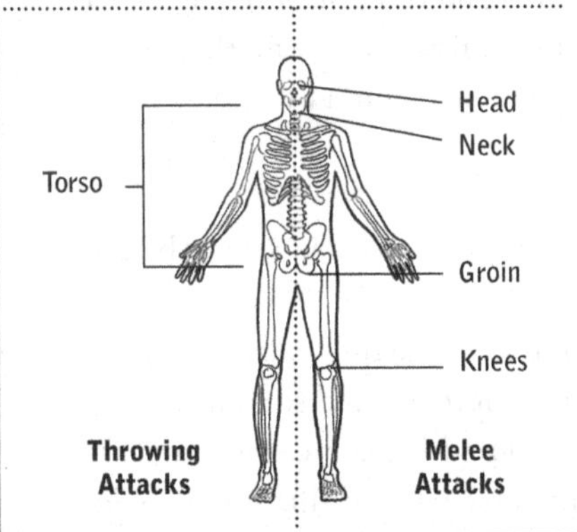
Head
Neck
Torso
Groin
Knees
Throwing Attacks
Melee Attacks

COA 3: Use as melee weapon.

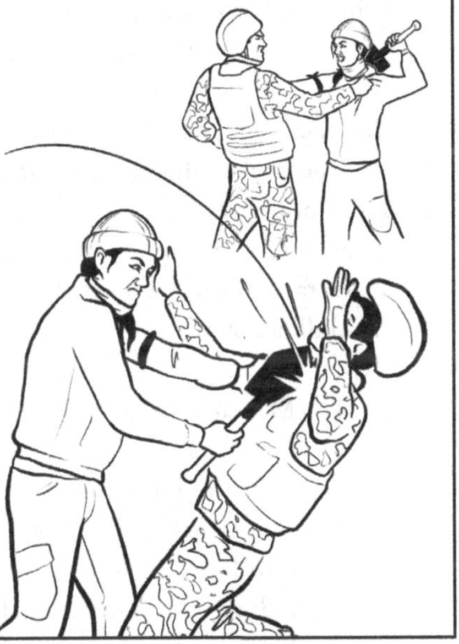

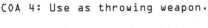

COA 4: Use as throwing weapon.

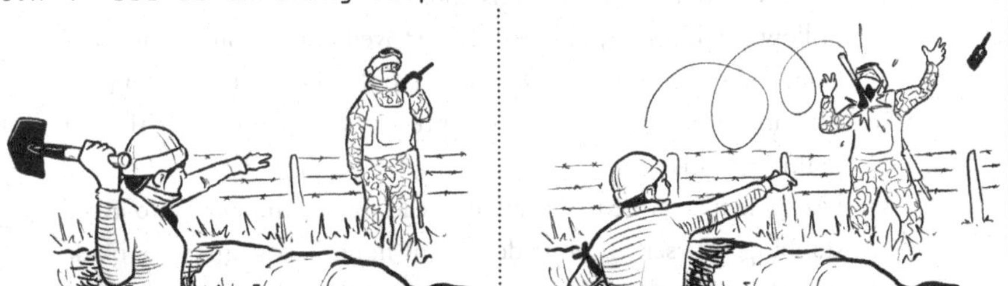

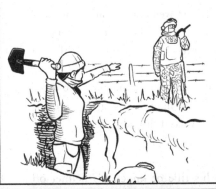

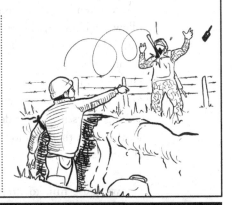

BLUF: One tool to rule them all.

For informational purposes only,
exercise caution, prioritize safety, and obey all laws.

ELIMINATE A SENTRY

Using a suppressed weapon to stalk a sentry is always the preferred option, but if one isn't available, it can be accomplished manually.

In most situations, the sentry will be wearing a helmet and body armor, carrying a rifle, and have comrades within shouting distance.

The stalker should make the attack silently wearing rubber soles, dark clothing, balaclava, gloves, and carrying no equipment other than a pistol and knife. "Jump test" your gear to eliminate anything that could shake, rattle, or make noise. Your face and hands should be camouflaged (see skill no. 003).

1. Maneuver to a position within three feet of the sentry before springing to attack.
2. With the fingers and thumb of your left hand fully extended, strike him across his throat with your left forearm and simultaneously stab him beneath his ribs and below his plate carrier into his kidney with your knife. The initial blow to the throat will make him gasp for air and unable to scream. The shock of the kidney strike will render him unconscious.
3. Follow the blows by the very fast movement of your right hand from the small of his back, over his right shoulder, and cupping his mouth and nose. This will prevent him from breathing or making a noise.
4. Use zone discipline (three zones: head, torso, and pelvis) to avoid stabbing yourself. If your dominant hand is engaging the blade into the torso, then nondominant hand should be in the head or pelvic zone, etc.

If the blows cause him to drop his rifle or knock his helmet off his head, don't make any effort to catch them. Should this happen, do nothing, but remain motionless for ten seconds. Afterward it is unlikely than anyone will come to investigate.

No. 029: Eliminate a Sentry

CONOP: The most important targets are well guarded with sentries.

COA 1: Move silently until you are in a position three feet behind the sentry.

COA 2: Spring forward and attack the sentry's throat with the bone of your left forearm as you simultaneously knife him beneath his rib cage and into his kidney.

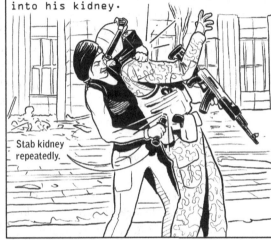

Stab kidney repeatedly.

COA 3: Leave the knife in his kidney and move your right hand around to cup his mouth and nose.

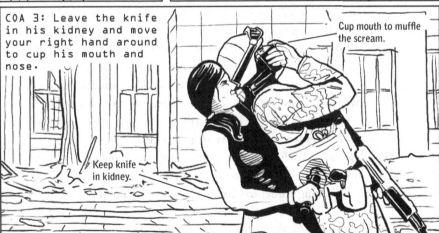

Keep knife in kidney.

Cup mouth to muffle the scream.

BLUF: Death is seldom silent, but with practice can be controlled.

For informational purposes only,
exercise caution, prioritize safety, and obey all laws.

BREACH A DOOR

House-to-house combat often requires breaching doors. Time is always a factor, and you don't want to give anyone on the other side additional time to prepare a defense.

Determine the weakest part of the door. If it opens away from you, the weakest part of the door will be just above or below the primary lock (often part of the handle). Most inner doors are hollow core and easy to break. However, exterior doors are often solid core and require more effort. Metal doors may require additional tools. If the hinges are on the outside, the door will open toward you and will be nearly impossible to breach manually.

There are three types of breaching.

1. Mechanical: For most hollow-core doors that open inward, a swift mule kick just above or below the lock, or a blow with a sledgehammer or battering ram, will force it open. A hydraulic spreader or Halligan tool ("Hoolie") can also be used to break the lock or the door.

2. Ballistic: Kinetic breaching uses a projectile weapon to breach an opening. The best results are with a shotgun firing buckshot or birdshot. Attacking the latch and lock is easiest and requires fewer shots, whereas attacking the hinges will require additional shots. Place the muzzle in contact with the door and angled the shot downward at a forty-five-degree angle.

3. Explosive: This is the most dangerous technique and is potentially slower than a ballistic breach. However, it but may be necessary for breeching hardened sites such as concrete bunkers.

No. 030: Breach a Door

CONOP: Urban combat requires citizens to be able to force open closed or locked doors.

COA1: Anatomy of a door

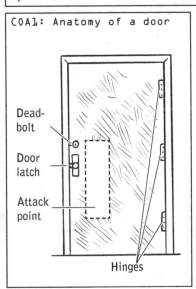

Dead-bolt

Door latch

Attack point

Hinges

COA2: Mule kick: Stand with your back one foot from the door. Bend at the waist, shift your weight to your standing leg and raise the other foot. Kick with your knee slightly bent and the flat of your foot striking the area just below the handle.

COA3: Crowbar: Insert into the door jam and leverage to force the door open.

COA4: Ballistic: Place the muzzle in contact with the door, or as close as possible, and angled downwards at a 45-degree angle.

BLUF: You'll never need to knock.

NO. 031

VENTILATOR STABBING TOOL

When operating in nonpermissive environments (NPEs), you may not be able to carry your concealed pistol or edged weapon and need a tool for personal protection. Carrying one in your shirt pocket may save your life.

Hi-tech carbon fiber ventilator knives are rigid, extremely hard, and may save your life in a crisis. Because they aren't metallic, they don't set off security alarms, and with the addition of a plastic end cap, they appear to be ordinary disposable pens.

To survive, you must violently stab the attacker in the neck or throat to create a brief opportunity for escape. Wrap a handkerchief or add a rubber eraser to the back of the pen to avoid injury to your striking hand. After your initial strike, immediately slam the pen with the palm of your other hand to drive it deeper into the attacker. The shaft becomes a spigot.

You can craft a ventilator pen using the shaft of a carbon fiber arrow, a Dremel tool, and the end cap from a disposable plastic pen. Carbon fiber arrows can often be sourced in even remote destinations.

To craft the ventilator pen, do the following:

1. Use the cutting disc on your Dremel tool to cut the arrow into multiple six-inch tubes. Have adequate ventilation and wear a mask.
2. Cut a thirty-degree angle to sharpen one end.
3. Use a barrel tip on your Dremel to narrow the tip and add a belly.
4. Add a plastic cap/pocket clip and carry it in your shirt pocket almost anywhere you go (except on an airplane).

No. 031: Ventilator Stabbing Tool

CONOP: Conceal a fighting tool in your uniform or kit for use in an emergency.

COA1: Gather a carbon fiber arrow, Dremel tool, and the end cap from a disposable plastic pen.

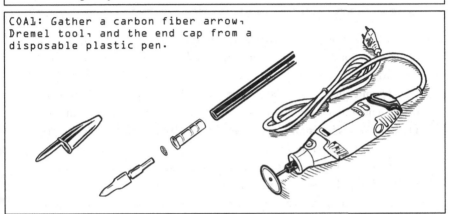

COA2: Cut a 30-degree angle to sharpen one end.

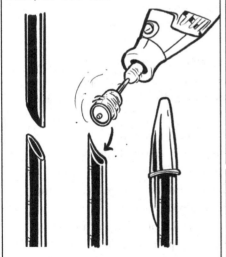

COA3: Use a barrel tip on your Dremel to narrow the tip and add a belly.

COA4: Add a plastic cap/ pocket clip and carry it in your shirt pocket.

Remove cap to stab target.

BLUF: Stab in the neck or throat to bleed them out.

For informational purposes only, exercise caution, prioritize safety, and obey all laws.

LEATHER PISTOL BELT

Leather belts exist to support equipment for weapons or first aid. Think of a holster for your pistol/secondary, pistol and rifle mag pouches, and first aid kits.

Beyond these two needs, everything else on your belt is mission dependent, and a knife, flashlight, and multitool are common additions. Dump pouches for empty magazines are popular as well, but it is a matter of available space on the belt.

Avoid putting too much gear at the front in case you need to hit the deck and stay close to the ground.

A sturdy leather belt can is versatile and can be a lifesaver. Avoid synthetic belts with plastic (composite) buckles and select a heavy leather belt that will be more resistant to cutting, tearing, and stretching. Your buckle should be solid with a long prong for security.

Other operational uses for your belt include the following:

1. Tourniquet or sling: Use your belt in an emergency to stop blood loss, cradle an injured arm or shoulder, or tighten a splint.
2. Buddy drag: Evacuate a buddy who can't walk while under hostile fire.
3. Rescuing people: Pull a buddy from a raging river.
4. Brass knuckles: Wrap several times around your hand for a leather boxing glove with a short blackjack attached.
5. Breaking windows: Wrap the belt around your palm and whip the buckle to break a car side-window.
6. Sharpening a knife: Use the reverse side of the belt as a strop.
7. Hoist: Pull someone or something up or down or use as a tow rope.

No. 032: Leather Pistol Belt

CONOP: A strong leather belt can perform many more tasks than carrying essential gear.

COA 1: Select a heavy-duty leather belt with a sold buckle and long prong.

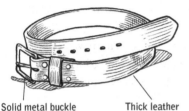

Solid metal buckle w/ long prong

Thick leather

COA 2: Sharpening a knife

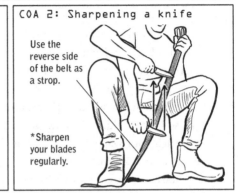

Use the reverse side of the belt as a strop.

*Sharpen your blades regularly.

COA 3: Buddy Drag

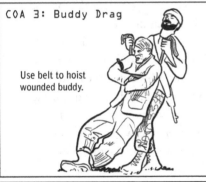

Use belt to hoist wounded buddy.

COA 4: Breaking Windows

COA 5: Protect Knuckles

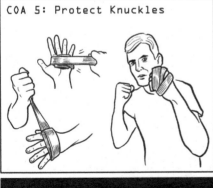

COA 6: Restrain Prisoner

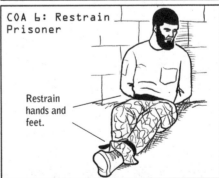

Restrain hands and feet.

BLUF: Everything you wear supports your mission.

For informational purposes only, exercise caution, prioritize safety, and obey all laws.

NO. 033

MINI WATER PURIFIER

In combat more men die from disease and sickness from microbes than from bullets. And while weapons and gear are considered your first priorities for combat, they may not be as important to your survival as clean drinking water.

Fortunately, with some preparation you can craft a mini water purifier for use in the field. Mimic the filtration system used by Mother Nature and wash your water over and through rocks, pebbles, sand, twigs, and charcoal (burned wood).

Start with a container, like a two-liter plastic soda bottle that will hold sand and rocks. This container must have a large hole at the top and a smaller opening at the very bottom to let the clean water out.

Place a layer of fabric in the bottom of the container. Then place a layer of charcoal, followed by layers of sand, grass, and gravel. Pour the dirty water in at the top and the filtered water drips out at the bottom.

This method of water filtration can even make muddy water drinkable. However, an improvised water filtration system will not remove waterborne pathogens, such as bacteria and viruses. Boil the water if possible or consider adding a water purification tablet, some drops of iodine, chlorine, or bleach for additional protection.

No.033: Mini Water Purifier

CONOP: A source of clean drinking water may be more important to your survival than guns or gear.

COA1: Acquire the 2-liter plastic soda bottle, a knife, and some sand, grass, gravel, charcoal, and cloth.

COA2: Cut off the base of the soda bottle.

COA3: Stuff cloth into the screw-cap end of the bottle. Alternate layers of charcoal, sand, grass, and gravel.

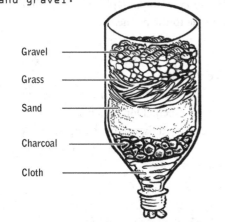

- Gravel
- Grass
- Sand
- Charcoal
- Cloth

COA4: Pour dirty water in the top and wait for the clean water. Remember to boil the clean water or use additives to kill water-borne pathogens.

- Dirty water
- Filter
- Filtered water

BLUF: You'll die in three days without water.

SMARTPHONE SPY MIRROR

Taking discrete photographs of enemy personnel and equipment places your life at risk. By crafting a disposable spy mirror, you'll be able to take covert photographs when you phone is pointed straight ahead or at a right angle away from the target.

You'll need a thin piece of stiff cardboard, a small mirror from a lipstick tube, glue, and some duct tape.

You should do the following:

1. Photocopy the outline from the book and cut it out.
2. Paste the outline onto a piece of thin cardboard and cut away the excess material.
3. Glue a small mirror, approximately one inch by one inch, to the center of the cardboard and fold along the sides.
4. Use duct tape to mount the mirror housing on the face (front) of your smartphone camera.
5. Activate the front facing camera on your phone.
6. The mirror can be mounted to take photographs when pointed straight ahead or at a right angle to the phone.

You can mount the mirror over the camera lens to photograph straight ahead or at a ninety-degree angle to either side.

Mount the mirror onto the face of your smartphone camera just before the clandestine photograph(s) are to be taken. Don't keep it mounted on your phone any longer than is necessary. Dispose of the mirror lens apparatus as soon as possible, upload the images to a discreet web site, and erase the images from your smartphone.

No. 034: Smartphone Spy Mirror

CONOP: If you are apprehended taking covert photographs of military personnel or equipment you may be executed as a spy.

COA1: Acquire a thin piece of stiff cardboard, a small 1" square mirror from a lipstick tube, glue, and some duct-tape.

COA2: Photocopy the spy mirror outline from this book and cut it out.

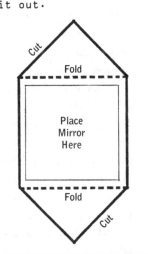

COA3: Paste the outline onto a piece of thin cardboard and cut away the excess material.

COA4: Glue a small mirror, approximately 1" by 1", to the center of the cardboard and fold along the sides.

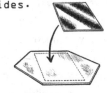

COA5: Use duct tape to mount the mirror housing over the front facing lens of your smartphone.

BLUF: Dispose of the spy mirror and wipe the photos as soon as they have been uploaded.

For informational purposes only,
exercise caution, prioritize safety, and obey all laws.

NO. 035

COVERT SMARTPHONE TACTICS

Citizen soldiers are only one part of a large "shadow army" of clandestine supporters living inside the occupied areas. The presence this network of agents and informers makes the occupiers nervous and boosts the morale of those trapped under their rule.

Members of the resistance can play an important role in tracking enemy troop and equipment movements as well as identifying collaborators for retribution after the war. Agents use both hobby drones and cell phone cameras to send covert photos of potential enemy target to the military. Each image file contains metadata, including the creation date and geographic location data showing where the photo was taken. Armed with this uploaded information, the military can sometimes destroy the targets within a few hours.

The shadow network of agents also keeps a record of neighbors who have switched sides to help the occupiers. The residences of these collaborators should be photographed and sent to the military so that they can't later make false claims that they were with the resistance. Marking the homes of collaborators with wanted posters and graffiti also raises morale and discourages others from selling out the resistance.

Agents in the shadow war must realize that if discovered taking photographs of military targets, they may be executed as spies. As such, it is essential that agents learn how to take photographs covertly and without attracting attention. As soon as possible, the images should be uploaded to a designated web site and removed from the user's phone. Having them discovered at a checkpoint search could cost you your life.

For informational purposes only,
exercise caution, prioritize safety, and obey all laws.

No. 035: Smartphone Tactics

CONOP: Members of the resistance can provide photographs of enemy personnel and equipment for rapid targeting.

COA1: Use your phone settings to enable photos to be taken with the volume button.

COA2: Learn to conceal your phone in a pocket, backpack, or book. Use video mode to collect imagery.

COA3: Let your hand naturally hang by your side as you walk pass a target and take photos with the volume button.

COA4: As you drive past a target place your hand on the top of the passenger seat in a relaxing manner as you hold the camera pointed out the passenger window. Take covert photos with the volume button.

BLUF: Suspicious behavior will be detected long before anyone notices the camera.

For informational purposes only,
exercise caution, prioritize safety, and obey all laws.

Basic Precautions

To take a covert photo with a smartphone, first do the following:

1. Disable sounds on your phone so that the tell-tale shutter sound will not be heard when an image is taken. This can usually be done by flipping the volume mute button.
2. Disable the flash so that it can't go off under any circumstances.
3. Confirm that your metadata is being recorded for each photograph for intelligence use.
4. Rather than taking individual photos that might attract attention, leave the camera on and recording images in high-resolution video mode automatically as you surveil the target. You can later recover single images from individual frames of the video.

Hide Your Phone

Next, conceal your phone so that it will remain unseen. Because the only part of your smartphone that needs to be visible is a small opening for the camera lens, the rest of the phone can remain hidden in a backpack, shirt pocket, or even a book.

Hold Your Phone Nonchalantly

Practice holding your phone down by your side as you walk, or on the top of the passenger's seat as you drive, when passing by a target. Record in high-resolution video mode the entire time and grab individual frames later for individual images. Other times you can pretend to be texting as you cradle the phone in your hand in a nonsuspicious manner as you twist your wrist and point the lens toward the target.

You can also create a simple right-angle mirror to place over your camera lens and point your phone away from the target as you take discreet photos (see skill no. 034).

NO. 036

SABOTEUR'S VEST

During wartime, one of the most effective weapons in any country's arsenal is sabotage: attacking an invader's war engine by crippling key supplies, manufacturing, strategic locations, and even logistic routes. Saboteurs are most effective when they aren't obvious and remain invisible to the visible enemy. Depending on their skills and training, they may be operating alone or as members of the organized resistance.

The challenge for saboteurs is to be able to access the sabotage location, plant the device, and withdraw to a place of safety before the act is discovered and without getting caught. Doing so requires training and preparation. Crafting a saboteur's vest allows the soldier to efficiently organize and transport his tools and the explosive/device in a self-contained vest beneath his coat while leaving his hands free. The clandestine portable workspace carried in the vest makes it easier to install the sabotage device and abort the operation with all your tools in an emergency (see skill no. 037).

To create the saboteur's vest, you'll need a standard fisherman's vest with retractable clips and the tools listed below:

- multitool (attached to retractable reel); we recommend the Leatherman Military Utility Tool (MUT)
- multimeter small (attached to retractable reel)
- liquid solder
- electric tape
- covert entry tools
- red lens (LED) head lamp or small flashlight with red lens
- extra latex gloves
- Faraday lined pocket for cell phone
- explosives and fuse (carried in rear pocket)
- magnifying reading glasses (for use in low-light conditions)
- clandestine portable workspace (see skill no. 037.)

No. 036: Saboteur's Vest

CONOP: An effective sabotage operation requires training, preparation, and the ability to swiftly locate your tools in the dark.

COA1: Saboteur's Vest

4x3 in MICA cards

Liquid solder

Multi-tool

Multi-meter

Red lens head lamp

Faraday lined pocket for cellphone

Ring key blanks

Explosives and fuse

Electric tape

Rare earth magnets

Cotton gloves

Magnifying reading glasses

Clandestine portable workspace

Fly fishing vest

PORTABLE CLANDESTINE WORKSPACE

Clandestine entry operations require preparation, stealth, and having a plan for when everything goes wrong. Whether you are covertly searching a room, copying documents, manipulating a safe, installing a listening device, or planting a sabotage device, your security can change in an instant if your mission is compromised or your presence is detected. As such, withdrawing rapidly without leaving a trace of your activity becomes essential.

The biggest impediment to a rapid exit is gathering the tools and materials where you are working. Fortunately, with a portable clandestine workspace, your work area is limited and defined, and by simply pulling the two handles together, the workspace (and your tools and materials) collapses like a "hobo's bag" and can be quickly carried away.

To make one you'll need a three-foot circle of burlap (or other heavy cloth), two kneepads, some grommets, paracord, and duct tape.

1. Lay out the burlap circle and install a grommet every twelve inches around the circumference.
2. Thread 550 Paracord through the grommets and create two opposing handles with duct tape.
3. Mark the handles with fluorescent paint to spot them easily in the dark (see skill no. 025).
4. Rivet (or sew) the two kneepads into place on the burlap.
5. Sew two red LED lights onto the burlap to illuminate the work area.

If you need to abort, don't waste time stowing gear. Instead grab and lift the two handles to collapse everything (tools, explosives, etc.) into the hobo bag as you quickly exit according to your escape plan.

No. 037: Portable Clandestine Workspace

CONOP: Clandestine operations must be conducted so that they can be aborted quickly without leaving a trace.

COA1: Acquire three-foot circle of burlap (or other heavy cloth), two knee pads, some grommets, para cord, and duct tape.

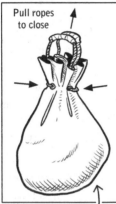

Pull ropes to close

COA2: Lay out the burlap circle and install a grommet every 12" around the circumference.

COA3: Thread 550 Para cord through the grommets and wrap two opposing handles with duct tape.

COA4: Mark the handles with fluorescent paint to spot them easily in the dark.

COA5: Rivet (or sew) the two knee pads into place on the burlap.

COA6: Sew two red LED lights onto the burlap to illuminate the work area.

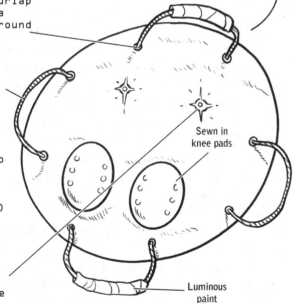

Sewn in knee pads

Luminous paint

BLUF: Nothing gets left behind.

ESCAPE BY SEA

Coastal waters are hard to protect due to several factors, making it a challenging task for authorities. The vastness of the oceans, the constant changing tides, and the numerous entry and exit points make it difficult to monitor every access point along the coastline. Coastal waters are also subject to international laws and regulations that restrict the use of certain surveillance techniques and further limit the control of illegal activities. The dynamic and vast nature of coastal waters, combined with technological advancements, legal limitations, and inaccessibility, make it tough to protect.

Cross-border operations (exfil or infil) during a conflict require planning and preparation. However, if you are stranded behind enemy lines, some general rules will help you select an escape route.

First, it is easier to pass or evade a newly created border checkpoint than one that is long-standing and hardened. And second, borders involving water crossings are traditionally more porous than land crossings, and a newly created checkpoint abutting an open body of water (large lake or sea) will be the most desirable to evade.

It is much easier to patrol on land than water, and patrol boats have difficulty spotting individual swimmers at night. Use underwater swim strokes to avoid splashing, and talk only in whispers.

In preparation for a water crossing, you'll need to cache an escape kit containing the following:

- a wetsuit to keep you warm in cool or cold water and avoid hypothermia
- swim mask and googles
- four five-gallon plastic jugs painted black and roped together to rest on while suspended between them
- waterproof compass and red light

No. 038: Escape by Sea

CONOP: Borders involving water crossings are traditionally more accessible than land crossings.

COA1: Acquire a wet-suit, fins, swim mask, compass, flashlight with a red lens, and dry bags.

COA2: Rope four 5-gallon plastic jugs (painted black) together, and create a sling between them to support your body.

COA3: Swing out 150 yards, or past the surf line before moving parallel to the coast.

COA4: Once you are safely past the border, swim to the closest light onshore.

COA5: Change into your dry clothes and conceal your escape gear.

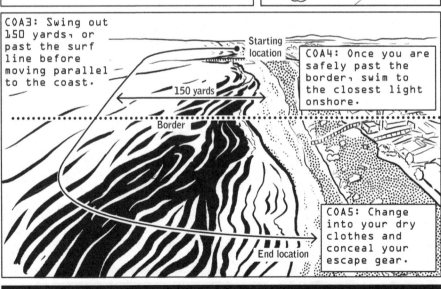

Starting location

150 yards

Border

End location

BLUF: Waterways are more difficult to patrol and safer for an escape.

- dry bag containing clothes, maps, and papers (roped to your leg)
- weapons and other gear that should be carried in a second dry bag lashed to one of the plastic jugs

Depart in the early evening hours and swim out 150 yards before moving parallel to the coast. Once you are safely past the checkpoint, look for lights to guide you to the nearest village. Once on shore, change onto your dry clothes and conceal your escape gear.

WATERBOARD PREPARATION

If you find yourself about to be waterboarded, something has gone wrong, very wrong, and someone wants information that you either don't have or are unwilling to provide.

Waterboarding is a form of drowning, and unless water is cleared from your nose, mouth, and throat soon enough, you will die from a lack of oxygen. If someone wants information from you, however, they'd prefer to keep you alive. Unfortunately, accidents happen, and you can drown in the process.

To be waterboarded, you are placed on your back, blindfolded, arms and legs restrained, head tilted downward, and a dry cloth placed over your mouth and nose. Then water is poured continuously onto the cloth. Though you can breathe at first, when the cloth gets wet, only the water gets through. Being afraid causes you to breathe rapidly, and once the oxygen is cut off, you gag and are about to pass out. A good interrogator will stop at that point and question you. However, if you don't provide answers, the cycle starts again. Though the process may sound simple, it's terrifying.

Understanding what's about to happen can help you survive, but there's only so much that you can withstand. Though you can delay providing information as long as possible, you'll eventually give in, or you'll die.

Here's what you can do to prepare:

1. Use situational awareness!
2. Don't be an easy target.
3. Commit to never be captured.
4. Never quit fighting!
5. Escape at the first opportunity.

Note: The US waterboarded military trainees in escape and evasion and anti-interrogation courses until the 1990s. Even though the students knew what to expect, it was a highly unpleasant experience.

No. 039: Waterboard Preparedness

CONOP: Waterboarding has been used for hundreds of years to recreate the sensation of drowning to extract information.

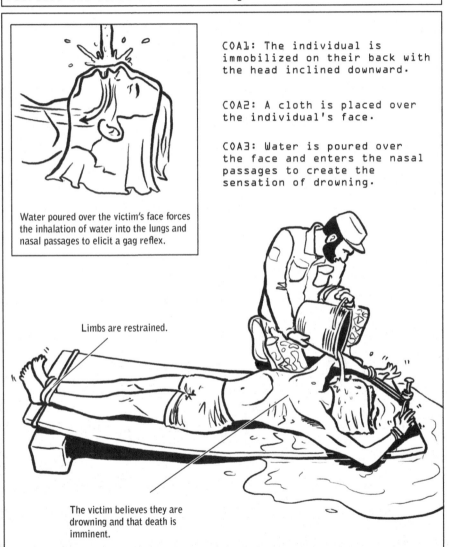

Water poured over the victim's face forces the inhalation of water into the lungs and nasal passages to elicit a gag reflex.

COA1: The individual is immobilized on their back with the head inclined downward.

COA2: A cloth is placed over the individual's face.

COA3: Water is poured over the face and enters the nasal passages to create the sensation of drowning.

Limbs are restrained.

The victim believes they are drowning and that death is imminent.

BLUF: Never, never, never, give up or quit fighting.

For informational purposes only, exercise caution, prioritize safety, and obey all laws.

2
SMALL
UNIT
TACTICS

FIGHT AS A UNIT

Citizen soldiers are more efficient and deadly when operating in five-man squads or fire teams. Citizen soldiers perform significantly better in combat against invaders because they fight for each other and for their homeland.

A fire team is the smallest fighting unit and may operate autonomously, or with other citizen soldiers. Only in a highly unusual circumstance would a fighter operate alone, and never from an exposed position such as in the middle of a street.

In defensive positions, the team can cover up to the range of its weapons or the limits of visibility, whichever is less.

A typical fire team consists of three to five soldiers and would be made up of the following:

Team Leader

The team leader is responsible for controlling the tactics of the fire team, such as their objective, exact positioning, rate of fire and ammunition, medical levels, and communicating with other citizen soldiers. His primary weapons are his assault rifle and radio.

Sniper

The sniper is responsible for establishing an overwatch position and identifying and eliminating threats at longer distances. His primary weapon is his sniper rifle.

Specialist

The specialist may serve as the spotter for the sniper or be trained as a demolitions specialist for sabotage operations. His primary weapon is his assault rifle.

**For informational purposes only,
exercise caution, prioritize safety, and obey all laws.**

No. 040: Fight as a unit

CONOP: Resistance fighters are more efficient and deadly when fighting in 5-man fire teams.

COA1: Operate together as a unit, and never fight alone.

Radio for Comms

Binoculars

Med kit

Assault rifle

1. Team Leader

Ghillie Suit (Based on terrain)

Sniper rifle w/ scope

2. Sniper

Javelin anti tank weapon

Spotting scope

Assault rifle

3. Specialist

Assault rifle

Shovel

Grenades

Extra magazines

4. Rifleman

Shears

Med kit

Assault rifle

5. Rifleman

For informational purposes only,
exercise caution, prioritize safety, and obey all laws.

Rifleman

The rifleman is responsible for the security of the team. His primary weapon is his assault rifle.

Rifleman (Support)

The rifleman provides security of the team and is also responsible for bringing ammunition and supplies to the team. His primary weapon is his assault rifle.

COA2: Fight only from prepared fighting defensive positions and never from exposed locations such as the middle of a street.

1.	Team Leader
2.	Sniper
3.	Specialist
4.	Rifleman
5.	Rifleman

Mouse Holes

COA3: Use concrete and rubble to make yourself invisible to the enemy and mouseholes to move between rooms and buildings.

COA4: Have a planned escape route from every fighting location.

BLUF: Citizen Soldiers operate as cohesive teams and support each other.

For informational purposes only,
exercise caution, prioritize safety, and obey all laws.

HAND SIGNALS

Hand signals on the battlefield are an essential aspect of military communication. Soldiers must operate in a variety of conditions where they may not always be able to communicate over the radio or other electronic devices. In these situations, using hand signals can be the most effective way to communicate. Here are some reasons why the importance of using hand signals on the battlefield cannot be understated.

Firstly, hand signals are silent, which is important for ensuring stealth and maintaining the element of surprise during a mission. Verbal communication can be heard by the enemy, giving away the position and mission of the soldiers. Hand signals, on the other hand, allow soldiers to communicate without alerting the enemy.

Secondly, hand signals can be used when electronic equipment fails. In situations where electronic equipment fails, such as when batteries run out or in areas where electronic communication is impossible, soldiers can rely on hand signals to communicate important information.

Thirdly, hand signals can be used in noisy environments. The battlefield can be loud, with gunfire, explosions, and other noises making it difficult to hear verbal communication. Hand signals provide a means of communication that is not reliant on hearing.

Lastly, hand signals are universal and can be understood by soldiers of different nationalities and languages. Soldiers from different countries may not speak the same language, but hand signals can provide clear and concise instruction that is easily understood by all.

In conclusion, using hand signals on the battlefield is a crucial aspect of military communication. It allows for stealth operation, can be used when electronic equipment fails, is effective in noisy environments, and provides universal communication. Soldiers should be trained in the use of hand signals as part of their training, ensuring effective communication during missions.

No. 041: Hand Signals

CONOP: Communicate with hand signals to maintain noise discipline.

COA1: Useful hand signals:

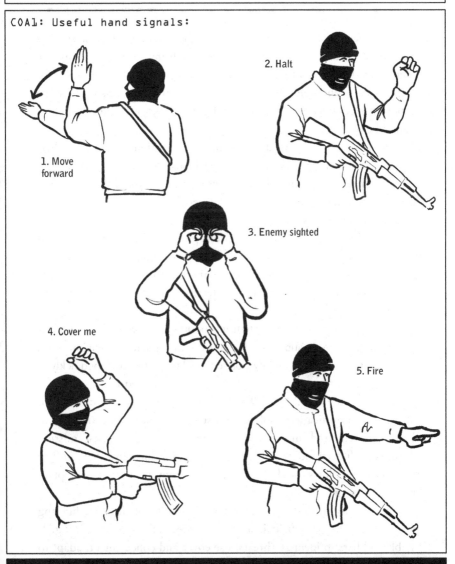

1. Move forward

2. Halt

3. Enemy sighted

4. Cover me

5. Fire

BLUF: The middle finger is the only hand signal reserved for the enemy.

FIGHTING POSITIONS

The battlefield is a dynamic and ever-changing environment, and soldiers must have an understanding of different fighting positions to operate effectively. Understanding different fighting positions is crucial for both offensive and defensive operations. Here are some reasons why the importance of understanding different fighting positions on the battlefield cannot be overstated.

Firstly, understanding different fighting positions provides soldiers with a clear understanding of the battlefield and enables them to identify potential threats. Knowing the positions of the enemy and their potential movements allows soldiers to make informed decisions about selecting the optimum fighting position.

Secondly, different fighting positions provide soldiers with cover and concealment. Cover offers protection from enemy fire, while concealment provides soldiers with the ability to remain hidden. Understanding these positions allows soldiers to use them effectively in offensive and defensive operations.

Thirdly, knowing different fighting positions allows soldiers to adapt quickly to changing situations. The battlefield is an unpredictable environment, and situations can change rapidly. Soldiers need to be able to adapt quickly to changing circumstances and use different positions as needed.

Lastly, understanding different fighting positions is crucial for effective communication. Soldiers must communicate effectively with their teammates and superiors to coordinate efforts and achieve mission objectives. Understanding different fighting positions and their unique characteristics allows for clear and concise communication to take place more quickly and efficiently.

In conclusion, understanding the importance of different fighting positions on the battlefield is a crucial aspect of military training. It enables soldiers to identify threats, use cover and concealment, adapt to changing situations, and communicate effectively with their teammates. Soldiers must be trained in the use of different fighting positions to ensure successful outcomes in the field of battle.

No. 042: Fighting Positions

CONOP: Fighting positions are environment dependent and selected to provide optimum cover and concealment.

COA1: Standing

Press rifle butt into shoulder to steady weapon.

Feet shoulder width apart

COA2: Crouching

COA3: Prone

COA4: Kneeling

COA5: Behind Cover and or concealment

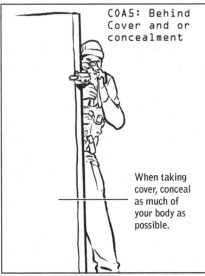

When taking cover, conceal as much of your body as possible.

BLUF: Always mislead the enemy as to the true location of your positions and strength.

For informational purposes only,
exercise caution, prioritize safety, and obey all laws.

NO. 043

SMALL UNIT PATROLLING

Military units are tasked with patrolling various areas to ensure the safety and security of the region. These patrols are conducted in a systematic manner and follow a predetermined set of guidelines and procedures.

Before initiating a patrol, the unit leader will gather information about the area that needs to be patrolled. This information includes the terrain, possible threats or obstacles, and the expected duration of the patrol. They will then formulate a plan for the patrol that includes the route to be taken, the number of citizen soldiers required for the patrol, and any necessary equipment needed for the mission.

Once the plan is in place, fighters will set off on its patrol. Citizen soldiers typically move in single-file formations, with the point man always on the lookout for threats or signs of danger. The rest of the unit follows closely behind, maintaining a distance that allows for quick communication and reaction time.

As the patrol moves through the area, fighters may encounter natural or man-made obstacles. In such situations, fighters must clear the area before the patrol continues to ensure that no surprises suddenly appear from behind. If the patrol detects any threat, citizen soldiers take cover and get ready for combat.

A critical aspect of patrolling is maintaining operational security at all times. This means that citizen soldiers must avoid being detected by enemy forces while on patrol. Soldiers, therefore, should keep a low profile, communicate with hand signals, and avoid the use of any electronic gear that may give away their position. Remember technology is not always your friend, and if it allows your enemy to track you, it will get you killed.

No. 043: Small Unit Patrolling

CONOP: Learn to move as a team while maintaining weapon discipline, fields of fire, and stealth.

COA1: Patrol in single file alternating firing positions.

Point Man   Patrol Leader   Comms   Medic   Rear Security

COA2: Use specialty teams to assess obstacles.

Man made

Natural

COA3: Keep a low profile and use hand signals to communicate.

BLUF: Sleep with the sun, move with the moon.

CONDUCT RECONNAISSANCE

A reconnaissance mission is a critical operation that involves gathering vital information about an enemy's intentions, capabilities, and resources. The following are steps to conduct a successful reconnaissance mission:

1. Plan the mission. Before conducting a recon mission, proper planning is essential. Factors like the operational goal, team composition, equipment needed, and infiltration (infil) and exfiltration (exfil) routes to be considered.

2. Conduct a risk assessment. Assess the risks associated with the mission and devise measures to mitigate them. The go/no go criteria from insert to extract should be considered, discussed, and option determined.

3. Gather intelligence. Before the operation, gather information on the area of interest, such as maps, aerial photos, satellite imagery, and open-source information about terrain, weather, and enemy presence. The more you know, the better the plan.

4. Deploy the team. Deploy the recon team to the area of interest. Ensure they are equipped with appropriate gear, such as navigation equipment, first aid, communication gear, and weapons.

5. Conduct reconnaissance. Conduct a thorough reconnaissance of the area of interest using binoculars, scopes, and cameras to gather information about the enemy.

6. Monitor enemy movements. Monitor enemy movements, patterns, and routines in case of any changes or new developments.

7. Document the reconnaissance. Document and gather all the information and intelligence using the SALUTE reporting format (see skill no. 045).

8. Return to base safely. Ensure the team returns to the base safely with their information.

Conducting a reconnaissance mission is essential when fighting for freedom. Through meticulous planning, a committed team, and dependable equipment, a successful mission becomes an attainable objective.

No. 044: Conduct Reconnaissance

CONOP: Intelligence gathering missions that are not compromised increase the likelihood of future mission success.

COA1: Gather Intelligence about the enemy.

COA2: Infiltrate enemy lines.

COA3: Setup Operational Observation Point

Use a star formation to protect all sides of the unit.

Conduct reconnaisance

COA4: Return to designated exfil vehicle without being detected.

BLUF: Eyes and ears before the fist.

NO. 045

SALUTE REPORT

The military's use of the SALUTE report is an effective communication tool that enables soldiers to relay vital information rapidly. The SALUTE report is a standardized method used to report information about the enemy, their location, movement, and strength. The report is initiated by the use of a correct military salute, followed by a brief exchange of information regarding the critical elements of the enemy's situation. This information is then forwarded to higher headquarters, enabling commanders to make informed decisions and plan appropriate courses of action. The use of the SALUTE report has been proven successful in combat situations and is widely taught and practiced in military training to ensure soldiers are equipped with the communication skills necessary to carry out their mission successfully.

A SALUTE report is a military acronym that stands for size, activity, location, unit, time, and equipment. It is an important tool used in the military for gathering and reporting intelligence and information about enemy forces or potential threats.

The purpose of a SALUTE report is to provide a clear and concise format for the description of the target or situation being observed, allowing military personnel to accurately analyze and respond to the information. The report provides critical details, such as the size of the target, what activity the target is engaged in, the location of the target, the unit or organization the target belongs to, the time of observation, and any relevant equipment or weapons. One SALUTE report provides valuable tactical information. Multiple SALUTE reports from different reconnaissance missions provides valuable strategic intelligence.

In summary, a SALUTE report is a standardized method of reporting information that helps citizen soldiers gather and analyze intelligence, plan operations, and make informed decisions on and off the battlefield.

No. 045: SALUTE Report

CONOP: Use SALUTE to standardized reporting and ensure proper intelligence collection.

COA1: Size

Small

Medium

Large

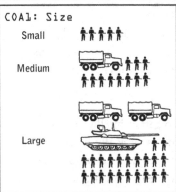

COA2: Activity

COA3: Location

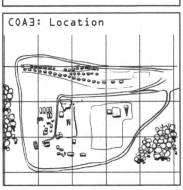

COA4: Unit Type

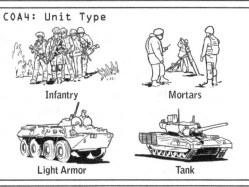

Infantry   Mortars

Light Armor   Tank

COA5: Time Frame

COA6: Equipment

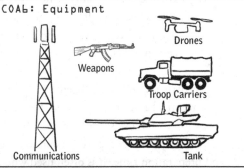

Drones

Weapons

Troop Carriers

Communications   Tank

BLUF: Knowing is half the battle.

For informational purposes only,
exercise caution, prioritize safety, and obey all laws.

CONDUCT RAIDS

Military raids can be used for a variety of purposes, including intelligence gathering, hostage rescue, and targeted strikes against enemy positions. There are several different types of military raids, each with its own specific objectives and techniques.

- Reconnaissance raid, which is used to gather intelligence about an enemy position. This type of raid is typically carried out by small teams of highly trained citizen soldiers who gather information about enemy troop movements, fortifications, and other key details.
- Direct action raid, which is used to eliminate a specific target, such as a high-value enemy leader or an enemy main supply route. These raids are often carried out by citizen soldiers and can involve vehicles, other fighters, and other specialized equipment.
- Sabotage raid, which are used to damage or destroy enemy infrastructure, such as bridges, roads, and communication lines. This type of raid is often carried out by highly trained teams of engineers and can be highly effective in disrupting enemy logistics and communications.
- Hostage rescue raids, which are used to free hostages from enemy hands. These raids are often highly complex, involving specialized teams of negotiators, intelligence gatherers, and highly trained commandos.

Whether used for intelligence gathering or direct action, military raids play a critical role in modern warfare and require careful planning and execution to achieve success.

A hasty raid is typically conducted quickly with limited planning and preparation time. It is often used when immediate action is required, such as when attempting to rescue hostages or seize a strategic location. Due to the limited planning time, hasty raids can be risky and may have unpredictable outcomes.

No. 046: Conduct Raids

CONOP: Utilize violence of action to take down an enemy target.

COA1: Reconnaissance Raid

Gather intelligence regarding key details.

Collect all electronics.

COA2: Direct Action

Eliminate specific targets.

COA3: Sabotage Raid

Destroy infrastructure

COA4: Hostage Rescue

Free hostages being held by enemy.

BLUF: Combat is fast, unfair, cruel, and dirty.

A deliberate raid, on the other hand, is a well-planned and coordinated operation that involves exhaustive planning, reconnaissance, and preparation. The objective of a deliberate raid is to achieve the mission objective at minimal risk to personnel and equipment. Deliberate raids are often used in large-scale ground operations, such as when attacking an enemy stronghold or when conducting a targeted assassination.

NO. 047

VEHICLE INTERDICTION

Conducting a vehicle interdiction is an essential skill set for every citizen soldier. The objective of a vehicle interdiction is to stop a particular vehicle that may be transporting individuals or cargo that pose a significant threat to citizen soldier security.

The first step in conducting a successful vehicle interdiction involves gathering intelligence. Teams must identify potential targets and develop a comprehensive plan to interdict the vehicle while minimizing risks to the team.

The planning stage should include comprehensive route analysis, traffic patterns, and identifying potential escape routes. It's also crucial to coordinate with law enforcement officials where the vehicle will be stopped to minimize collateral damage.

Secondly, specialized equipment should be used to interdict the vehicle. This equipment should be designed to stop a car without killing its occupants. Common equipment used in vehicle interdictions includes spike strips and caltrops (see skill no. 083).

During the interdiction, the team should be poised for decisive action once the vehicle is immobilized. Teams must maintain situational awareness and be prepared to engage in any potential threats that may arise.

Conducting a successful vehicle interdiction requires an effective intelligence gathering process, rigorous planning, and sometimes improvised equipment—all of which must be combined with the right mindset, training, and expertise. Citizen soldiers must be agile and adaptable to changing circumstances, react quickly to potential hazards, and maintain seamless communication throughout the operation. A well-executed vehicle interdiction operation can save lives and prevent significant security breaches.

No. 047: Vehicle Interdiction

CONOP: Intercept and engage a moving vehicle in order to collect intelligence or capture the enemy.

COA1: Planning should include route analysis, traffic patterns, and identifying potential escape routes.

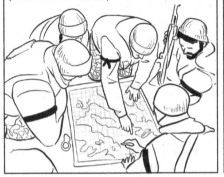

COA2: Acquire equipment for prisoner acquisition.

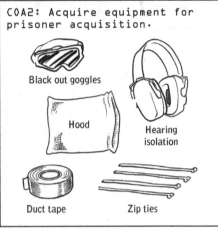

Black out goggles

Hood

Hearing isolation

Duct tape

Zip ties

COA3: Use the Police Intervention Technique (PIT) to stop the vehicle without killing the occupants.

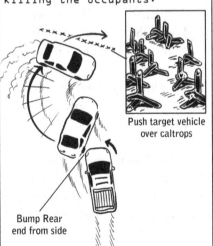

Push target vehicle over caltrops

Bump Rear end from side

COA4: Collect prisoner using restraining equipment.

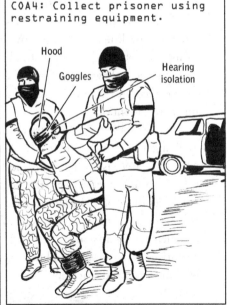

Hood

Goggles

Hearing isolation

BLUF: Channelized areas are good, but choke points are better.

For informational purposes only, exercise caution, prioritize safety, and obey all laws.

INSERTION, INFILTRATION, AND EXTRACTION

Citizen soldiers insert and infill to a target with precise techniques that ensure stealth and surprise. The key is to approach the target undetected, with minimal noise and a low profile. Citizen soldiers are trained to use a variety of methods to accomplish this, including aerial-, ground-, and water-based infiltration techniques. These methods are tailored to the specific needs of the mission and the terrain in which the target is located.

In aerial infiltration, citizen soldiers use helicopters, planes, or drones to drop onto a target area. This method is often used when the target is located in remote, rugged terrain, or the area is difficult to access. One of the key advantages of aerial infiltration is that it allows the troops to get to the target quickly and with minimal noise.

In ground infiltration, citizen soldiers move on foot or in vehicles, either by sneaking through enemy lines or using unconventional routes to approach the target. This method requires extreme physical fitness and excellent tactical awareness. It is often used when the target is located in a populated area where the use of a helicopter or aircraft might attract unwanted attention.

Citizen soldiers can also use water-based infiltration techniques, such as diving or coming ashore from a boat. This method is particularly useful when the target is located on or near the coast or in areas where rivers, lakes, or other waterways provide access.

Regardless of the method used, citizen soldiers undergo rigorous training to ensure that they can infiltrate their target undetected and complete their mission successfully. Proper training ensures that these operatives have the skills and tools necessary to accomplish their mission with precision and efficiency.

No. 048: Insertion and Extraction

CONOP: Determine means of clandestine transportation to and from target area.

COA1: Use aerial infiltration to land in remote areas in enemy territory.

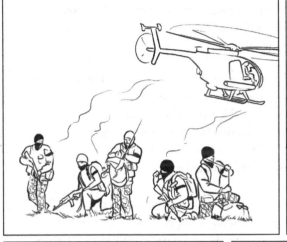

COA2: Once team is inserted, use ground transportation to move undetected towards the target.

COA3: Once the mission is completed, the team needs to be extracted quickly and efficiently away from danger.

High capacity vehicle waiting for extraction

COA4: Use maritime vessels like a Zodiac to exfil away from land and towards safety.

Zodiac

BLUF: Get in and out, emphasis on out.

For informational purposes only, exercise caution, prioritize safety, and obey all laws.

NO. 049

CONTACT FRLR

The response of a citizen soldier to an enemy ambush depends on various factors, such as the size of the ambush force, the weapons available, and the terrain. However, some general guidelines that a soldier may follow in such a situation are the following:

- Take cover. Find a secure location, such as behind a barrier or in a depression, to provide cover from enemy fire.
- Assess the situation. Quickly determine the size and location of the enemy force, and identify any friendly forces nearby.
- Call for reinforcements. Use communication devices to call for backup, providing details about the situation and the enemy's position.
- Return fire. If able, engage the enemy with accurate and controlled firepower, focusing on known or suspected enemy positions.
- Move to a better position. If necessary, reposition to a more advantageous location, either alone or as part of a coordinated effort with friendly forces.
- Evacuate casualties. If necessary, secure and evacuate any injured or wounded soldiers, prioritizing those who are in immediate danger.

It's important to remember that responding to an enemy ambush is a complex and dynamic situation that requires quick thinking, proper training, and the ability to adapt to changing circumstances. Contact drills are tactics that military soldiers use to respond to an enemy threat during combat. Some common types of contact drills include the following:

- Immediate action drills: These are preplanned responses to specific enemy actions, such as an ambush or a sudden enemy attack. They are executed quickly and without hesitation.
- Fire and movement drills: This involves coordinated movement and firing by soldiers to advance on an enemy position. One team provides covering fire while the other team moves, and then they switch roles.

No. 049: Contact FRLR

CONOP: Fields of fire must be established to effectively engage an enemy while protecting the team against an attack from the rear.

COA1: Guns pointing Front, Right, Left and Rear.

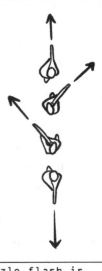

COA2: Incoming shots heard

COA3: Fighters hit the ground in the direction of their rifle barrel.

COA4: Muzzle flash is seen from tree line.

COA4: Fighters turn to engage.

BLUF: Always protect your six.

For informational purposes only,
exercise caution, prioritize safety, and obey all laws.

- Boundary drills: These are used when a unit is moving in a formation and makes contact with the enemy. The unit immediately halts and establishes a perimeter to protect itself and return fire.
- Break contact drills: These drills are used to disengage from an enemy force and move to a more secure location. They typically involve covering fire from one team while the other team withdraws.
- Squad attack drills: These drills involve a small unit, typically a squad, working together to take on an enemy position. The squad coordinates its movement, firepower, and support elements to overcome the enemy.

It's important to note that contact drills are practiced regularly in training so that soldiers can respond effectively in real-life situations. Additionally, the specific drills used can vary based on the unit's tactics, weapons, and operational environment. The reaction of soldiers to enemy contact and gunfire will depend on the specific situation, their training, and the tactics used by their unit. However, some general guidelines that soldiers may follow in such a situation are the following:

- Take cover. Find a secure location, such as behind a barrier or in a depression, to provide cover from enemy fire.
- Return fire. If able, engage the enemy with accurate and controlled firepower, focusing on known or suspected enemy positions.
- Communicate. Use communication devices to inform other members of your unit about the situation and enemy location.
- Follow established drills. If applicable, follow established contact drills, such as immediate action drills or fire and movement drills.
- Maintain situational awareness. Continuously assess the situation, including enemy locations, friendly forces, and potential danger areas.
- Reevaluate and adjust. If necessary, adjust your position, firepower, and tactics to overcome the enemy and maintain an advantage.

It's important to remember that reacting to enemy contact is a complex and dynamic situation that requires quick thinking, proper training, and the ability to adapt to changing circumstances.

AMBUSH

A military ambush is a surprise attack by a small military force against a larger one. There are several different types of ambush formations that military units can use, including the following:

1. Linear ambush: A linear ambush involves soldiers positioned in a straight line, either parallel or perpendicular to the enemy's expected line of movement. This type of ambush is effective for disrupting enemy movement and limiting their options for escape.

2. L-shaped ambush: An L-shaped ambush involves soldiers positioned in two lines, forming an L shape, with one line parallel to the enemy's expected line of movement and the other perpendicular to it. This type of ambush is effective for both disrupting enemy movement and providing flanking fire.

3. V-shaped ambush: A V-shaped ambush involves soldiers positioned in a V shape, with the base of the V facing the enemy's expected line of movement. This type of ambush is effective for channeling the enemy into a confined area and limiting their options for escape.

4. Box ambush: A box ambush involves soldiers positioned on all sides of the enemy, creating a boxlike perimeter. This type of ambush is effective for trapping the enemy and limiting their options for escape.

5. Ambush with a killing zone: An ambush with a killing zone involves soldiers positioned to create a large, open area in which the enemy is vulnerable to concentrated fire. This type of ambush is effective for inflicting significant casualties on the enemy.

It's important to note that the specific ambush formation used will depend on the unit's tactics, weapons, and operational environment. Additionally, military units may use a combination of ambush formations or modify them to fit their specific needs.

No. 050: Set an Ambush

CONOP: An ambush uses concealment, stealth, and surprise to attack and destroy an unsuspecting enemy.

COA1: Linear Ambush: Fighters positioned in a straight line, either parallel or perpendicular to the enemy's expected line of movement.

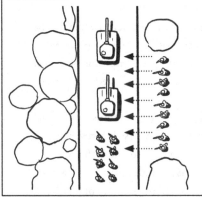

COA2: L-Shaped Ambush: Fighters positioned in two lines, forming an L shape, with one line parallel to the enemy's expected line of movement and the other perpendicular to it.

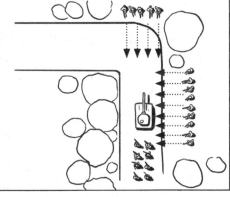

COA3: V Shaped Ambush: Fighters positioned in a V shape, with the base of the V facing the enemy's expected line of movement.

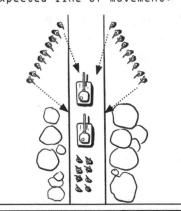

COA4: Box Ambush: Fighters positioned on all sides of the enemy, creating a box-like perimeter.

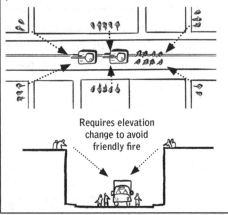

Requires elevation change to avoid friendly fire

BLUF: Walk away from a fight and set an ambush.

BUTTONHOOK AMBUSH

The buttonhook ambush serves as an excellent countertracking technique when faced with pursuit from an adversarial force. This tactical maneuver not only enables you to ascertain if you are being followed but also provides an opportunity to launch a surprise attack on the stalking enemy. As the name suggests, it involves executing an aggressive movement away from the adversary, swiftly creating distance between both parties. Subsequently, you execute a slow and gradual J-turn, catching the opposing force off guard. In a matter of moments, they find themselves subjected to a barrage of fire they never saw coming.

This technique is particularly effective in snowy terrains, where the white surroundings aid in concealing your movements. However, it can also be employed in forested or jungle environments, albeit with increased challenges. Navigating swiftly through dense jungles poses its own set of difficulties, but with careful planning and execution, the buttonhook ambush can still be a valuable tactic to disorient and engage the enemy.

By employing the buttonhook ambush, you gain the advantage of surprise, disorienting the pursuers and swiftly turning the tables in your favor. It demands precise coordination within your team, ensuring seamless execution and effective communication. When implemented with proper planning, this tactic can prove instrumental in outmaneuvering and neutralizing a stalking force, increasing your chances of mission success.

No. 051: Button Hook Ambush

CONOP: Use your own tracks to confirm and kill your pursuers.

COA1: Create tracks for you enemy to follow while using a subtle J turn to double back and observe their movement.

Resistance fighters

Observe and engage if necessary.

Field of view

J turn

Enemy movement

Foot path

Jungle tracking

Snow tracking

BLUF: Not all tracks get you caught.

For informational purposes only,
exercise caution, prioritize safety, and obey all laws.

MOBILE FIRE TEAM

Citizen soldiers riding fast and silent electric bikes (e-bikes) are ideally suited for reconnaissance and special operations. From setting night ambushes and launching attacks with drones to the deliberate sabotage of road and railway bridges, fighters use speed and silence for protection. Mobile citizen soldiers with an intimate knowledge of the towns and countryside create an advantage over a larger and less mobile adversary who is limited to using only larger roads and highways.

Portable antitank weapons can level the playing field for defenders, but only if the limited supply of weapons can be transported to firing positions and quickly relocated before the enemy can react. Fortunately, missile-carrying electric bikes help citizens quietly reach a firing position in less time than rucking in on foot and reduces their exposure to enemy tank and machine-gun fire.

A fire team raiding party on e-bikes can arrive at a site to pass instructions to local fighters, pick up or drop off weapons, or set an ambush. If they're spotted, they can speed off much faster than most foreign forces can follow. They can also make use of muddy and hilly terrain that is unavailable to the enemy's lumbering, armored vehicles.

The e-bikes speed and "small signature" (minimal sound and thermal image) allows them to chase down enemy forward observers and snipers and prevent ambushes. The e-bikes are also too light to trigger many of the booby traps and special mines designed to allow civilian traffic to pass unharmed but detonate when a heavy armored vehicle passes. In an emergency, e-bikes can even be used to drag rakes in search of roadside bombs.

No. 052: How to Create a Mobile Fighting Unit

CONOP: Using speed and maneuverability to bypass obstacles and identify threats is an essential skill.

COA1: Electric motor bikes provide speed of movement and silence.

COA2: Identify the threat and call-up bikes with NLAW missiles to destroy the target.

COA3: Delfast TOP 3.0 72V/48 Ah 3000W Dual Suspension Electric Mountain Bike

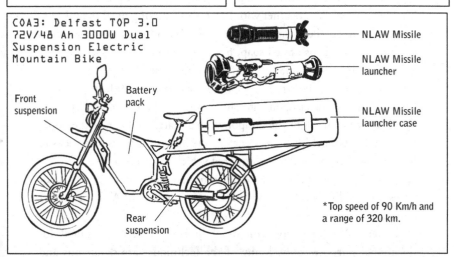

Front suspension

Battery pack

Rear suspension

NLAW Missile

NLAW Missile launcher

NLAW Missile launcher case

*Top speed of 90 Km/h and a range of 320 km.

BLUF: Mobile fighting units carry a deadly punch.

For informational purposes only,
exercise caution, prioritize safety, and obey all laws.

MOLOTOV NAPALM COCKTAIL

Molotov cocktails were first used in the 1930s in Spain to fight against a stronger military with more soldiers, tanks, and planes. The cocktails, or "burn bottles," were improvised incendiary weapons that consisted of a glass bottle filled with flammable substances and equipped with a fuse. In use, the fuse was lit, and the bottle thrown, or dropped, to shatter against a target such as an armored vehicle. The flammable substance in the bottle is ignited upon contact and spreads as the fuel burns.

Molotov cocktails are typically used by outmanned fighters and are highly effective when thrown over a barricade or dropped from high buildings onto vehicles. They are also effective in creating chaos as a diversionary tactic and demoralizing dispirited enemy troops confronted with house-to-house combat. They are nonattributable and can be assembled in advance from locally obtained items and stored or quickly assembled when needed.

Create napalm by slowly mixing equal amounts of grated soap and shredded polystyrene together with fuel oil and stirring until the mixture reaches a thin jellylike consistency. The Ukrainian formula is "three cups polystyrene, two cups grated soap, five hundred milliliters gasoline, one hundred milliliters oil, and one jumbo tampon fuse."

Any bottle or glass jar with a small neck can be used. Just fill it with napalm and cram a tampon into the mouth of the bottle as a stopper. When ready to use, light the tampon with a match and throw the bottle at the target. The gel-like consistency of the napalm spreads and sticks to the tops and sides of tanks and armored vehicles as it burns.

Note: Molotov cocktails are dangerous and may be illegal to make or possess in the US. Check with your local attorney and the ATF for further information.

Note: All information contained in this book is presented for educational purposes only. Many of the techniques are dangerous and should not be performed without training, supervision, and safety equipment, such as gloves, face mask, and eye protection. The authors,

No. 053: Molotov Napalm Cocktail

CONOP: Molotov cocktails can be prepared in advance and used to attack a stronger force.

COA1: Acquire: fuel-oil, gasoline, soap, polystyrene, tampon, glass bottle, and matches.

COA2: Slowly mix small parts of soap and polystyrene with the fuel-oil until they are gel-like and then mix with gasoline.

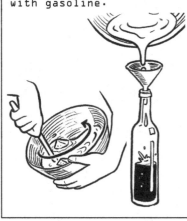

COA3: Plug the bottle with a fuel-soaked tampon.

COA4: Light fuse and throw.

BLUF: Molotov cocktails are fun battlefield beverages.

For informational purposes only,
exercise caution, prioritize safety, and obey all laws.

writers, editors, publisher, illustrator, and any other persons involved with this book are not liable for any damages, injuries, or legal actions that may arise from the use or misuse of any information contained herein. Always check the laws where you live and obey them. Don't do any harm and don't do any stupid stuff!

MOLOTOV COCKTAIL LAUNCHER

The Molotov cocktail (see skill no. 053) is a very effective weapon against armored vehicles when it can be dropped from high building onto unsuspecting armored vehicles. By creating a shotgun launcher for the Molotov cocktails, its effective range can be extended out to one hundred meters.

In his 1961 manual *Guerrilla Warfare,* Cuban revolutionary Che Guevara christened the improvised launcher as the "M-16" because it consisted of a sixteen-gauge sawed-off shotgun with a pair of legs added in such a way that they form a tripod. The weapon should be fired at an angle of about forty-five degrees; this can be varied by moving the legs back and forth to adjust the range. It is loaded with an open shell from which all the shot has been removed.

A cylindrical stick extending from the muzzle of the gun is used as the projector. A bottle of the Molotov cocktail mixture and flaming fuse is placed on a rubber base that is mounted on the end of the stick. This apparatus will project the burning bottles one hundred meters or more with a high degree of accuracy. It is an ideal weapon against an enemy who has used flammable materials in his defenses and for firing against tanks.

You'll need a Molotov cocktail bottle, twelve-gauge sawed-off shotgun (cylinder bore, no choke) and shell, wooden legs for tripod, wooden broomstick or dowel, two pieces of rubber, and a plastic soda bottle.

Note: Sawed-off shotguns with barrels shorter than eighteen inches, and overall length less than twenty-six inches, are illegal in the US unless first registered with the ATF and paying the $200 tax. Check with your local attorney and the ATF before proceeding. All information contained in this book is presented for educational purposes only. Many of the techniques are dangerous and should not be performed without training, supervision, and safety equipment, such as gloves, face mask, and eye protection. The authors, writers, editors, publisher, illustrator, and any other persons involved with this book are not liable for any damages, injuries, or legal actions that may arise from the use or misuse of any information contained herein. Always check the laws where you live and obey them. Don't do any harm and don't do any stupid stuff!

No. 054: Molotov Cocktail Launcher

CONOP: Molotov cocktails are even more effective when they can be launched at 100 meters against unsuspecting targets.

COA1: Acquire: Molotov cocktail bottle, sawed-off 12 gauge shotgun (cylinder bore, no choke), a shell without the shot, wood legs for tripod, wooden broom stick or dowel, two pieces of rubber, and a plastic soda bottle.

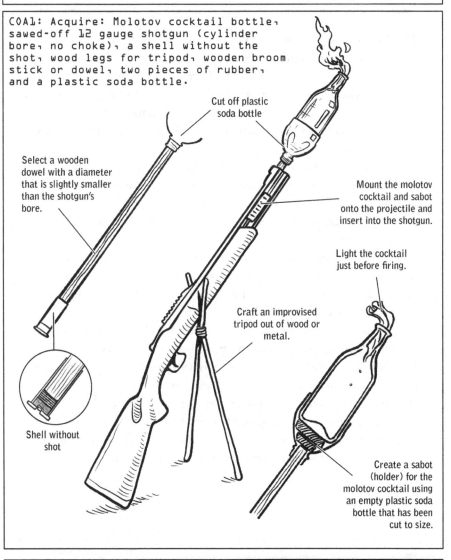

Cut off plastic soda bottle

Select a wooden dowel with a diameter that is slightly smaller than the shotgun's bore.

Mount the molotov cocktail and sabot onto the projectile and insert into the shotgun.

Light the cocktail just before firing.

Craft an improvised tripod out of wood or metal.

Shell without shot

Create a sabot (holder) for the molotov cocktail using an empty plastic soda bottle that has been cut to size.

BLUF: Molotov cocktails are unwelcome arrivals at any enemy gathering.

For informational purposes only, exercise caution, prioritize safety, and obey all laws.

MOLOTOV COCKTAIL ATTACK

Locally produced Molotov cocktails (napalm) can be effective against tanks and armored vehicles. Napalm cocktails burn at 1800 degrees Fahrenheit compared with the 1,000 degrees Fahrenheit temperature of gasoline cocktails. Once the fiery napalm strikes a vehicle, it spreads across the metal structure and sets fire to anything flammable or explosive. If any fire reaches the crew compartment, it will force evacuation even if it is extinguished.

Modern armored vehicles are less vulnerable if they are "buttoned up" with sealed hatches and openings. However, vehicle drivers and commanders often drive around with the hatches open for the improved visibility and general awareness it provides when compared with the very limited view through periscopes and vision blocks.

Coming under attack by Molotov cocktails forces the crew to "button down" and significantly reduces their ability to spot and deal with more serious threats. The fiery napalm cocktail is designed to generate clouds of smoke and several hits will have a cumulative effect.

Barricades and road obstructions should be strategically positioned to channel armored vehicles into a city along narrow streets with abutting high buildings. While Molotov cocktails are typically seen being tossed over barricades against the front and sides of oncoming armored vehicles, they are more effective when they are dropped from above.

Even if cocktail attacks against armored vehicles only serve to distract or partially blind the occupants, they become a much easier target for antitank teams armed with RPGs or other guided weapons.

No. 055: Molotov Cocktail Attack

CONOP: The hatches and openings on armored vehicles are vulnerable to attack.

COA1: Construct obstacles to channel tanks into a city along narrow roadways and tall buildings.

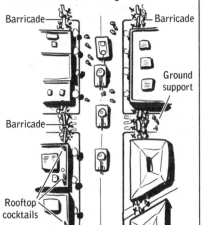

Barricade — — Barricade

Ground support

Barricade

Rooftop cocktails

COA2: Distract the tank with ground level fire as the molotov cocktails are dropped from above.

Rooftop cocktails

POP POP POP

RATATAT

COA3: Vulnerable Areas

1. Front hatch
2. Hatch
3. Gun tower
4. Hatch
5. Engine vent

COA4: Maneuver an anti-tank team into position to take out the tank.

BLUF: A distracted enemy is an easy target.

For informational purposes only,
exercise caution, prioritize safety, and obey all laws.

HOW TO MOUNT A SNIPER OVERWATCH

On overwatch, a sniper selects high ground or a tall structure to observe the terrain and identify enemy positions and movements. This vantage position allows him to provide covering fire for advancing citizen soldiers and is the first line of defense against enemy troops and approaching armored vehicles.

Overwatch is especially important when friendly forces are involved in urban operations and vulnerable to ambushes, car bombs, and enemy snipers on rooftops. The effectiveness of overwatch is not measured simply by the number of dead bodies and destroyed targets but also by its reassuring presence to friendly forces.

Depending on the mission and the size of the overwatch security team, the sniper may have multiple weapons including an assault rifle for close protection, a traditional sniper rifle for targets out to eight hundred meters, and the more powerful .50 caliber antimateriel/personnel rifle for targets beyond eight hundred meters. While all three weapons can kill people, only the .50 caliber rifles are vehicle killers.

Fifty-caliber rifles originated in WWI as antitank weapons to pierce through the armor of the iron tanks. Modern main battle tanks, however, have improved armor and are no longer vulnerable. However, improved .50 caliber armor-piercing/incendiary ammunition delivers three times the penetrating power of conventional rounds and is effective against the engine compartments of armored personnel carriers (APCs) and armored limousines from more than a half mile away.

The .50 caliber projectile is so powerful that it can punch clean through a cast iron engine block either crossways or lengthwise and is ideal for stopping suspected car bombers threatening soldiers.

No. 056: Sniper Overwatch

CONOP: Overwatch serves as the first line of defense against enemy troops and approaching armored vehicles.

COA1: Select high ground or a tall building to conduct overwatch.

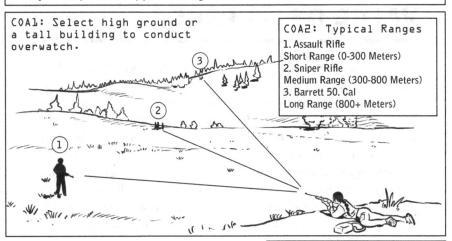

COA2: Typical Ranges
1. Assault Rifle
Short Range (0-300 Meters)
2. Sniper Rifle
Medium Range (300-800 Meters)
3. Barrett 50. Cal
Long Range (800+ Meters)

1. Assault Rifle: AK-47 (Short-Medium Range)

2. Sniper Rifle: Remington 700 (Medium-Long Range)

3. Sniper Rifle: Barrett .50 Cal (Long Range)

Typical Calibers

1) 7.62 x 39 mm
2) 7.62 x 51 mm NATO
3) .50 Cal

1 2 3

Aim for
Engine Bay

Use the .50 Cal Rifle as an
anti tank weapon

BMP-2 (APC)

BLUF: From a place you cannot see comes a sound you cannot hear.

PSYCHOLOGICAL VALUE OF SNIPERS

Due to the surprise nature of sniper fire, high lethality of aimed shots, and frustration at the inability to locate and counterattack snipers, sniper tactics have a significant negative effect on the morale of an invading force. Sniper tactics can be used to induce constant stress and fear in opposing forces, making them afraid to move about or leave cover and believe that death may arrive at any moment.

Snipers are an unseen terror that can inflict damaging psychological blows to enemy forces far disproportionate to their small numbers. This almost mythical status allows snipers to employ several psychological tricks to wreak further havoc with invading forces, including the following:

- Death should also be delivered by the sniper to those not engaged in combat and located in the rear lines where they should expect to feel safe. By denying them a place of refuge, the enemy increasingly perceives themselves to be surrounded and unable to rest and recover. Realizing that death can come at any moment is demoralizing, discouraging, and disruptive to military order and discipline.
- Regularly targeting invaders as they use the toilet, as opposed to when they are standing together, will also have a disproportionate reaction. Word of the practice will spread like wildfire and people will try to avoid using the toilet out of fear. Many will begin soiling themselves instead of risking death at the latrines. The odorific effect of this practice in the small confines of a tank or armored vehicle will be especially unpleasant.
- Break down the morale of the force each day by killing the man "on point" (in front of) on every patrol. This will make the assignment synonymous with a death sentence and severely affect morale and order.
- The sniper won't be able to kill all the people in the trench if they get out of it, but they can very, very reliably kill the first person. The psychological effect is that no one wants to get out of the trench to be the first person to die.

No. 057: Psychological Value of Snipers

CONOP: Use snipers to demoralize and demotivate the invading force.

COA1: Target enemy soldiers using the toilet to demoralize.

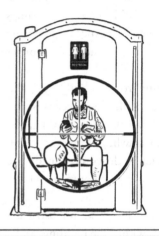

COA2: Target the first man in every enemy patrol to demoralize.

COA3: Kill soldiers resting in the rear lines to deny them safety and refuge.

COA4: Target the first person out of the trenches.

BLUF: No one rests well when death is on their doorstep.

For informational purposes only,
exercise caution, prioritize safety, and obey all laws.

NO. 058

MOUSE-HOLING

Mouse-holing is the essential urban warfare tactic in which citizen soldiers fight from prepared positions in single or multiple interconnected buildings while always remaining under cover. Well-prepared buildings serve as fortified bunkers to minimize the defender's exposure to enemy fire or observation and give them an advantage over numerically stronger adversaries.

Mouseholes provide access to adjoining rooms, buildings, and underground by blasting or tunneling through walls, floors, ceilings, and roofs. Small irregular openings in outside walls are used for shooting, and larger holes in the interior walls are used for crawling. Mouseholes can be created using explosives or simple tools such as the combat spade (see skill no. 027) and should comfortably fit a soldier so as not to clog traffic during a tense situation.

The ideal firing position will provide concealment, an unobstructed field of fire, protection against an attack from within the building, and a mouse-hole for a fast egress to the next firing position.

Steps to Create a Mousehole

1. Use your combat shovel to dig or enlarge a small loophole for firing.
2. Prepare sandbags to make your position defensible from both directions, should you be attacked from within.
3. Dig a larger mousehole in the closest wall, or floor, to serve as an egress path.

In some instances, a mousehole will be camouflaged with furniture, especially when they are created to aid a defending force or a clandestine operation. When used in defensive positions, mouseholes often join and combine with underground tunnels.

No. 058: Mouse-Holes

CONOP: Use prepared mouse-holes to move between fighting positions.

COA1: Dig a larger mouse-hole in the closest wall (or floor) to serve as an egress path.

COA2: Arrange sandbags to defend your position from attack from within.

COA3: Use your combat shovel to dig a small loophole for firing.

BLUF: Shoot through small mouse-holes, and crawl through the large ones.

MOTORBIKE HIT TEAMS

On November 27, 2020, Iran's top nuclear scientist, Mohsen Fakhrizadeh, was assassinated in a bold and unprecedented style of motorcycle assault outside Tehran. Reports indicate that a group of assailants operating under the guise of a marriage proposal planted explosives on a motorcycle, ambushed Fakhrizadeh's heavily armored vehicle, detonated the explosives, and shot at Fakhrizadeh's car with automatic weapons. The scientist was rushed to the hospital but succumbed to his injuries.

The brazenness and success of the Fakhrizadeh assassination raise concerns regarding a possible escalation of covert attacks in the future. The event could spark a new wave of tensions among Iran, Israel, and the United States.

High-profile targets are traditionally better protected where they sleep and where they work but become vulnerable when traveling by vehicle between the two.

Step 1: Study the target's daily travel routes and identify "choke points" where traffic is congested and regularly slows or stops. At these points, the target vehicle will be locked into position by the traffic and unable to maneuver. Motorbikes, however, can navigate among the stopped vehicles with ease.

Step 2: On the selected date, establish surveillance to send a text using a brevity code when the target's vehicle is in route. The MB driver serves as the spotter while the passenger is the communicator/shooter. Both are wearing dark clothing and motorcycle helmets to conceal their identities. The motorcycle is using a stolen license plate.

Step 3: As the target vehicle approaches the choke point and slows/stops in traffic, the MB team enters the traffic flow from behind. The team spots the vehicle and makes its approach from the six o'clock position.

Step 4: The MB team pulls alongside as the citizen fires multiple rounds at point blank range into the car using a suppressed small-caliber pistol and a brass-catcher to capture spent cartridges.

Or if the vehicle is armored, plant a small shaped-explosive charge with a time delay on the roof of the vehicle. The overpressure from the explosion will kill anyone inside. Afterward the motorbike continues ahead at a normal pace and is quickly lost in the traffic. The MB team takes the first exit and is far away before their adversaries can launch a response.

No. 059: Motorbike Hit Teams

CONOP: Mobile hit teams can use heavy traffic as cover to strike and escape quickly before an adversary can react.

COA1: Two Person Motorbike Hit Team

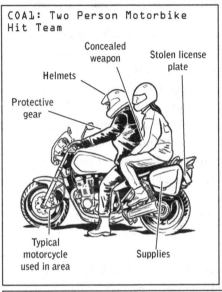

Concealed weapon

Helmets

Protective gear

Stolen license plate

Typical motorcycle used in area

Supplies

COA2: Approach target vehicle stuck in heavy traffic from the rear.

Target

Hit team

COA3: Tie bags around weapon.

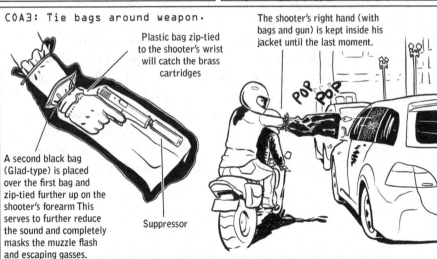

Plastic bag zip-tied to the shooter's wrist will catch the brass cartridges

A second black bag (Glad-type) is placed over the first bag and zip-tied further up on the shooter's forearm This serves to further reduce the sound and completely masks the muzzle flash and escaping gasses.

Suppressor

The shooter's right hand (with bags and gun) is kept inside his jacket until the last moment.

POP POP

BLUF: Speed, stealth, and surprise win every time.

For informational purposes only, exercise caution, prioritize safety, and obey all laws.

NO. 060

URBAN STRONGPOINTS

Strongpoints can be created by reinforcing buildings or using preexisting structures that are already hard to destroy such as heavy-clad concrete structures (e.g., government buildings, apartments, or banks). These buildings can become minifortresses or strongpoints within the city. If the defenders have the time, they can bring in sandbags and lumber to further harden the structure and create numerous bunkers and fighting positions.

Buildings must be carefully selected to become strongpoints and should offer multiple firing angles and an obstacle network that prevents attackers from simply bypassing or isolating the buildings to clear later.

Mines, wire, and other materials should be used to create obstacles around the building. Entryways should be sealed to make it difficult for the enemy to approach and enter the building without expending time, resources, and suffering casualties.

For example, a four-story apartment building overlooking a square with long lines of sight from three sides can be converted into an ideal strongpoint. Barbed wire and antipersonnel and antitank mines can be quickly placed around the building to limit access, holes cut into the inner walls to create walkways, and machine-gun firing points established in the building's corners. Interior access should be added to allow for rapid movement of defenders between floors and into the cellar.

Defenders will relocate to the cellar when the building is subjected to artillery fire and then to the top of the building or to higher floors when tanks and armored vehicles approach. Higher elevations allow antitank weapons to target the vulnerable thin roofs of personnel carriers and tanks.

No. 060: Urban Strong Holds

CONOP: Concrete structures like government buildings, apartments and banks can be converted into mini-strong holds.

COA1: Survey buildings and select well-built concrete structures to be reinforced.

COA2: Seal off lower entrances and surround the building with anti-personnel and anti-tank mines.

COA3: Create inner passageways on each floor and ways to rapidly move between floors and into the cellar.

COA4: Create protected machine-gun positions on the corners of the building.

BLUF: Create strong holds by reinforcing buildings that are already hard to destroy.

CLANDESTINE INTRUSION ALARM

Your campsite should be concealed from the enemy and protected at night with an intrusion alarm. Fortunately, you can improvise one using cotton thread and an inexpensive yo-yo style automatic fishing reel.

An automatic fishing reel is a mechanical device that retracts the line when the fish takes the bait and pulls the lure. To protect your campsite, run a line of cotton thread about four feet above the ground along the perimeter or across a trail. Tie the thread to a tree or bush and the other end to the extended line of the fishing reel about three feet before the end. Attach an empty soda can filled with a small rock to the end of the line. An intruder approaching your campsite will impact the thread, trip the automatic reel, and noisily retract the line and soda can.

Cotton sewing thread is available in sewing kits or on larger spools. For operational use, obtain several sewing bobbins and slide them onto a three-inch bolt with a nut on the end. Fill each bobbin with colored thread (neutral colors are usually best). When stretching the thread across a trail, tie one end to a tree and hold the bolt at both ends to allow the thread to unspool as you walk.

Positioning the winder, reel, and can within your campsite will reveal your location to an intruder. Instead, move the reel away from your camp but close enough to be easily heard at night.

No. 061: Low Tech Intrusion Alarm

CONOP: A clandestine alarm system will detect adversaries approaching under the cover of darkness.

COA1: Acquire bobbins or spools of cotton thread, 3" bolt and nut, "Yo Yo" reel, empty soda can, and small rock.

COA2: Place the bobbins on the bolt and load it with the cotton thread. You can carry multiple bobbins on a single bolt and hundreds of feet of thread.

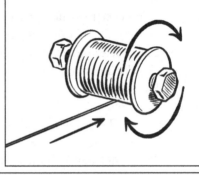

COA3: Tie the auto-reel to a tree or stick in the ground. Pull out the internal line as far as it will go and set the catch.

COA4: On the far side of the trail tie your thread about four feet up on a tree. Then unspool the thread as you walk across the trail to the location of the extended line form the reel.

COA5: Tie the thread to a point on the line about 3' before the loop at the end. Attach the can (with the rock inside) to the loop.

BLUF: Sleep with one eye open and one ear to the ground.

TACTICAL INTRUSION ALARM

Whether you're in a fighting position or at your base camp, an intrusion alarm system acts as an enemy deterrent by monitoring your perimeter to detect a stealthy and unexpected intruder. Use it to avoid being caught unaware.

Commercial solutions are expensive and may be unavailable, but during wartime you can scavenge an effective alarm system using a low-cost smoke detector, a clothespin, dental floss, some screw eyes, two metal thumbtacks, and some bits of wire and solder.

Here's how:

1. Smoke detectors have an external button that sounds the alarm when pressed to test the battery. Locate the test button contacts on the smoke detector circuit board and solder a three-foot piece of wire to both sides. When you touch the ends of the wire together, the alarm sounds.

2. Rig a standard clothespin with two opposing thumbtacks in the "jaws" so that they make contact when touching. Attach each of the wire leads from the smoke detector to one of the tacks. To keep them from grounding, place a small wedge-shaped wooden spacer between them.

3. Run your dental floss through screw eyes mounted around the perimeter of the area. Anchor one end of the floss to something solid, such as a tree or doorknob, and connect the other end to the wedge-shaped piece of wood holding the clothespin open.

4. Any intrusion into your space will displace the length of dental floss, pull out the wooden spacer, and set off the alarm!

No. 062: Improvised Intrusion Alarm

CONOP: A perimeter alarm system provides an early alert for enemy intruders.

COA1: Gather the components:

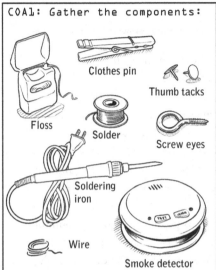

Clothes pin

Thumb tacks

Floss

Solder

Screw eyes

Soldering iron

Wire

Smoke detector

COA2: Rig a standard clothes pin with two thumb tacks and attach the wire leads from the smoke detector. A small spacer keeps them from touching.

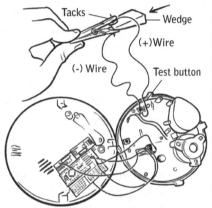

Tacks

Wedge

(+)Wire

(-) Wire

Test button

COA3: Run your dental floss through screw eyes mounted around the perimeter of the area and anchor it to something solid. Connect the other end to the small piece of wedge-shaped piece of wood keeping the clothes pin open.

Clothes pin shuts activating alarm.

COA4: The dental floss trip wire is almost invisible to an intruder… especially at night.

BLUF: Test the alarm system daily to confirm its operability.

NO. 063

CONCEALED OBSERVATION PERISCOPE

During the First World War, soldiers on the battlefield were spending most of their time inside trenches and underground shelters called dugouts. Such conditions posed special challenges related to observation. Sentries and snipers needed to be able to watch over no-man's-land to warn of enemy attacks, and artillery observers needed to be able to scrutinize enemy positions to identify targets and to gauge the accuracy of gunfire. As a solution, soldiers created trench periscopes by installing two mirrors at forty-five-degree angles at either end of a long box or tube to peek over the trenches.

More than one hundred years later, it is possible to covertly monitor enemy activity with camouflaged trail cameras (with Wi-Fi/Bluetooth) using an improvised version of the WWI periscope. The digital images are live, of excellent quality, and can be monitored wirelessly from your mobile phone or tablet (iPad, iPhone, or Android) in the safety of your fighting position. Some models are even equipped with low-light camera features that expand their usefulness.

Battery-powered trail cameras use a low-powered Bluetooth signal between your cell phone and the trail camera to remotely turn on/off the camera's Wi-Fi and save batteries. And because the trail camera generates its own Wi-Fi signal, your phone can be placed in the "airplane mode with Wi-Fi/Bluetooth turned on" to minimize your signal exposure.

Trail cameras can be mounted on a small board or stick and slowly raised or repositioned as needed. Depending on your environment, you can further refine the camouflage to be almost undetectable.

No. 063: Concealed Observation Periscope

CONOP: Resistance fighters need a safe and discreet way to observe enemy movements and positions.

COA1: You'll need a wireless trail camera, Velcro strips or paracord for mounting, a strip of wood or tree branch, and a mobile phone or tablet for monitoring.

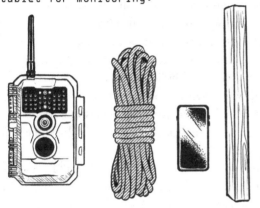

COA2: Secure the trail camera to the piece of wood so that it can be easily opened to change batteries.

COA3: Camouflage the wooden holder and camera to match your environment.

COA4: Place your phone or tablet on airplane mode, but and activate both bluetooth and WIFI on your cell phone or tablet.

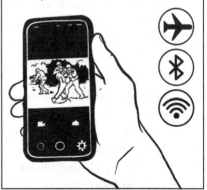

BLUF: Risk the technology not your people.

For informational purposes only,
exercise caution, prioritize safety, and obey all laws.

SHAPE THE TERRAIN

Armies usually attack urban areas with artillery, missiles, and aerial bombing before assaulting. As a result, buildings are partially turned into rubble. Concrete debris, however, can also be used as military-fortification material and provide the defenders with an important advantage.

Defenders have advantages over the attacking forces because of their local knowledge and greater control of the terrain. Not every building needs to be fortified to stop an attack, and buildings that are difficult to fortify may have greater value when they are converted into rubble. It is a very damaging process and an unfortunate reality of defensive warfare. However, it may add significantly to the defender's ability to shape the terrain to confront a larger invading force.

Rubble can be used to create physical barriers that are difficult for an invading army to navigate around or remove. Concrete and brick rubble are especially valuable for this purpose.

Defenders should initially create a plan to funnel attacking forces into prepared engagement areas and use rubble as obstacles to channel the attackers down a smaller number of avenues where they can be ambushed. Broken concrete, rebar, stones, bricks, or solid material is ideal for blocking roads and will significantly constrain the attacker's ability to operate and maneuver. Additional rubble may need to be created by destroying buildings at key locations to create fifteen-foot-high piles of rubble to block both the road and the enemy's direct line of sight.

Vehicles can be repositioned to block streets, furniture can be thrown into staircases, and concertina wire and remotely detonated explosive devices can be added to hinder easy movement between floors and into entryways of buildings. Concrete barriers, cars, buses, construction vehicles, dumpsters, furniture, and tires can be moved into streets and flipped over to channel, divert, or halt enemy armored fighting vehicles or dismounted personnel.

You can never have enough obstacles, and the process of adding to and reinforcing existing obstacles should continue as long as the threat exists.

Defenders should also develop creative methods of urban concealment

No. 064: Shape the Terrain

CONOP: Concrete rubble and debris can also be used as military grade fortification material.

COA1: Create a map of the city and identify the roads to be blocked to create channels for engagement and ambush.

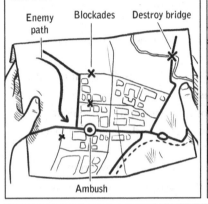

Enemy path | Blockades | Destroy bridge

Ambush

COA2: Create 15-foot-high obstacles from concrete debris to block key roads and side-streets.

COA3: Supplement barricades with old refrigerators, boilers, burning tires, vehicles, trucks, and even streetcars.

Burning tires

Barrels | Fridges + appliances

Burned out vehicles | Boilers

COA4: Use large sheets of cloth and metal on roofs and between buildings to foil drones and snipers.

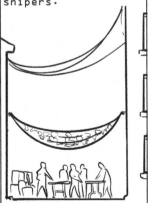

BLUF: Never stop fortifying or creating obstacles.

For informational purposes only,
exercise caution, prioritize safety, and obey all laws.

to hide obstacles, weapon systems, fighting positions, and movements. Simple solutions may include stringing large cloth sheets, metal, or tarpaulins on rooftops and between buildings to reduce sniper attacks. Sheets and tarpaulins should also be used to conceal fighting positions from the snooping eyes of drones overhead. While such defensive methods may sound primitive, they are disproportionately effective as a deterrent. If an enemy can't pinpoint defensive fighting positions, they can't concentrate their firepower on any single location.

If given enough time to prepare, do the following:

- Place many obstacles on main roads into cities and at dense points within urban areas.
- Construct and camouflage fighting positions inside buildings and near roadblocks for quick ambushes.
- Design and rehearse a series of alternate and supplementary positions, so-called "kill boxes," to unleash focused, violent attacks on isolated invaders.
- Create expedient "fallback routes" to shoot and move from those hasty ambushes to set up the next attack and draw in more invading forces.

NO. 065

CONFUSE AND MISLEAD INVADERS

Invading armies frequently rely upon road and directional signs for troop and vehicle movement. In urban areas the damage caused by artillery and missiles strikes often makes it difficult for invading armies to accurately determine street addresses.

Take the following steps as soon as possible to sabotage the invaders:

1. Remove all road signs with numbers and names of villages and cities to confuse the enemy. Store the signs so that they may be safely reinstalled after the war.

2. Alter existing road signs and signposts to point in the wrong direction at intersections or forks. The enemy may go the wrong way and travel miles before realizing his mistake.

3. In areas where traffic is composed of enemy autos, trucks, or convoys, remove danger signals from curves and intersections.

4. Add fake signs and distance numbers to point to notional cities and villages.

5. Add insulting political slogans to road signs to let the invaders know that they are unwelcome.

6. Tear down all signs with street and neighborhood names to cause disorientation to urban invaders and make it difficult to locate and arrest suspected citizen soldiers.

7. Remove all building numbers and building names.

8. Remove company names and advertising from buildings.

9. Remove all railroad station names.

The alteration or absence of a significant percentage of road signage will have the additional benefit of sewing distrust among invading troops who come to realize that all road signage can no longer be trusted.

No. 065: Confuse and Mislead Invaders

CONOP: The removal of road and directional signs disorients and confuses an invading army.

COA1: Remove all road signs with numbers and names of villages and cities to confuse the enemy.

COA2: Alter existing road signs and sign posts to point in the wrong direction at intersections or forks.

COA3: Add fake signs and distance numbers point to notional cities and villages.

COA4: Tear down all signs with street and neighborhood names to cause disorientation to urban invaders and make it difficult to locate and arrest suspected Resistance fighters.

BLUF: Don't make it easy for them.

NO. 066

HIDE FROM DRONES

Unmanned aircraft systems (UAS or drones) are used to detect and identify targets for other weapon systems to attack and kill. Avoiding detection requires the skillful use of camouflage and concealment to reduce your physical signature (visual, IR thermal, and radar) and disrupt the enemy's intelligence, surveillance, and reconnaissance efforts.

Advancements in surveillance cameras and facial recognition technology have made it easier for an occupying intelligence service to identify and track citizens who remain behind and attend demonstrations, protests, etc.

The way that you walk is also as unique as your fingerprint. Advancements in gait-recognition software and artificial intelligence (AI) have made it possible to identify and track walkers in the field or in demonstrations from surveillance drones.

Maintain a twenty-four-hour AirGuard in the field to detect the drones and initiate defensive actions. Some sophisticated UAS platforms will fly too high to be spotted form the ground. However, consumer/hobbyist drones are being deployed in greater numbers and fly low enough to be detected audibly or visually.

Hide yourself and your team in the field or at demonstrations and protests by employing the following tactics:

1. Camouflage everything: people, positions, walkways, and equipment to blend into the environment.
2. Operate in inclement weather (rain, fog, high wind, and dust) when drones cannot fly or cannot operate their sensors.
3. Find a concealed site and conform to the terrain, which is more reliable than bad weather. Find low dead ground and microterrain behind hills, alcoves, tucked against the shadows of buildings, or under trees or in tunnels. In the city, move inside a building.
4. Minimize your digital footprint. Avoid using wireless devices like mobile phones or GPS systems since they have digital signatures that can reveal your location.

For informational purposes only,
exercise caution, prioritize safety, and obey all laws.

No. 066: Hide from Drones

CONOP: Use camouflage and concealment to remain undetected by Unmanned Aircraft Systems (drones).

COA1: 2 person Hunter Killer Team for spotting UAS.

- Binoculars
- Search light
- Shotgun w/ anti drone rounds

COA2: Drones eye view of the battle field.

Camouflage vehicles + equipment

Hide under trees.

Hide between buildings.

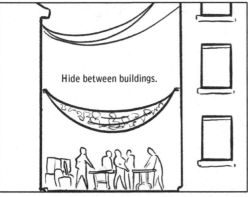

Hide under a ghillie blanket.

BLUF: Drones detect targets to be killed.

For informational purposes only,
exercise caution, prioritize safety, and obey all laws.

5. Disperse into multiple small elements that are easier to conceal.
6. Operate at night with NVGs (night vision goggles) to make it more difficult for the drone's cameras to see you.
7. Operate at dawn or dusk when shadows are long, sun glare is high, and the thermal crossover masks your heat signature.
8. Freeze if you detect a drone nearby. Never run as it makes it easier for the drone to detect you. Instead, go prone if you are on foot in the open. Avoiding looking up immediately and exposing shiny face. Cover all optics such as binoculars and rifle scopes.
9. Minimize your shadow and cover yourself with a Ghillie blanket. A space blanket will mask significant amounts of the body's temperature to evade thermal sensors.
10. Stay behind or under trees or in the underground. Put something between you and the drone. Stay inside if you are in the city. Stay away from the windows.
11. Disguise yourself to evade facial recognition software. Old-school disguise techniques, such as hats, glasses, masks, and scarves, go a long way toward scrambling drone-based facial-recognition software.
12. Evade gait-detection software by wearing extremely baggy pants to conceal leg movement or adding a small pebble into the heel of one shoe or a single knee brace to cause a pronounced asymmetrical limp.
13. Carry an umbrella with you to demonstrations or protests. They are ubiquitous and go a long way toward scrambling drone-based facial-recognition systems.

SABOTAGE AIRFIELDS

Airfields may prove even more important to an invading army than bridges, and allowing one deep within your territory to fall intact into enemy hands is a disaster. It is far better to destroy your own airfield and equipment than allow it to be used as an enemy beachhead behind your lines.

If the enemy is fast approaching and you have limited time for airfield destruction, the targets are listed below in order of their priority.

Runways and taxiways: Crater large craters with explosive charges in the middle (widthwise) of each runway, taxiway, and at hundred-yard intervals (lengthwise). Large craters that are not quickly repaired. However, if there is not adequate time to crater the runways, proceed to the remaining targets on the list.

Aircraft: Use thermite grenades to destroy the cockpit instrument panel and electronics. Use a standard grenade to blow off the tail of each aircraft.

Munitions: Use explosives to destroy all stockpiles of bombs and missiles.

Control tower: Smash all computers and communication equipment. If you have sufficient time, use explosive charges to topple the tower.

Generators: Use explosive charges to destroy the airfield's primary power station and standby generators.

Radar and navigation beacons: Use grenades to destroy.

Landing lights: Smash each landing light with a sledgehammer.

Service vehicles: Render all service vehicles inoperable with a thermite grenade in the engine compartment.

Hangars: Use explosive charges to bring down the roofs of all hangar-repair facilities. Leave booby traps inside any remaining structures.

No. 067: Airfield Destruction

CONOP: Allowing the enemy to capture an intact airfield deep within your territory can be disastrous.

COA1: Render all runways and taxiways inoperable by blowing large craters in the middle every 100 yards.

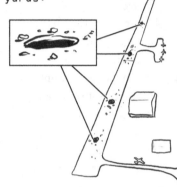

COA2: Render any remaining aircraft inoperable and demilitarize sensitive equipment onboard.

COA3: Destroy stockpiles of remaining munitions.

COA4: Smash all computers and communication equipment and use explosive charges to topple the tower.

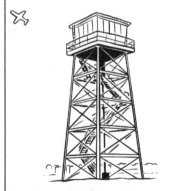

BLUF: Cratering the runways and taxiways is the optimum way to limit their use to the enemy.

NO. 068

SABOTAGE ROADWAYS

Roadways are essential for convoys moving vehicles, troops, equipment, and supplies. Stop the convoys, and the invading forces will run out of fuel and ammunition in a day or two of heavy fighting.

Convoys tend to follow a limited selection of routes since their heavy loads do not permit them to go off-road or across rough terrain. Because they travel slowly, they also generate significant dust and noise and are easy to spot using drones. Sometimes, even delaying a convoy can disrupt a timeline for resupply and render a unit combat ineffective. A small mobile fire team (see skill no. 040) can cause significant damage to a convoy with little risk to themselves.

To target a convoy, select a narrow choke point where topographic features (forest, rivers, gorges, etc.) force the vehicles to remain on the roadway. The following techniques can be employed:

- Use remote charges to detonate and block the first and last vehicles in the convoy.
- Prepare hidden traps in the roadway that are linked to trees prepared with explosive charges. Once tripped, the explosives cause the trees to fall and block the road.
- Plant mines below the roadsides to detonate under pressure from any vehicle that tries to escape.
- The presence of suspicious "fake" mines (see skill no. 090) will stop a convoy until sappers can investigate and clear the roadway.
- Have snipers deployed to target anyone attempting to exit their vehicles.
- Coordinate with mobile citizen soldiers to call in artillery or drones to coordinate the destruction of the convoy.

No. 068: Sabotage Roadways

CONOP: Convoys and extended supply lines are ripe for attack.

COA1: Identify chokepoints and bottlenecks for roadway attacks to trap the convoy.

Call in drones or rockets to destroy the trapped vehicles.

Explosive Charge fells tree blocking last vehicle

Deploy snipers to pick -off anyone exiting the vehicles .

Explosive Charge fells tree blocking roadway

Explosives for blocking the first and last vehicle in a convoy.

Sends signal to explosive

Spring Loaded

Land mines

BLUF: Starve the battlefield of food, fuel, and water.

For informational purposes only,
exercise caution, prioritize safety, and obey all laws.

SABOTAGE RAILROADS

The timely delivery of tanks, artillery, munitions, spare parts, soldiers, food, water, fuel, and medical supplies by rail will ultimately determine the victor in a conflict. Railroads and their related infrastructure are an essential resource to your adversary and are vulnerable to sabotage.

Signal cabinet disruption: Modern railroads utilize complex signaling systems (track circuits) to detect when sections of track are occupied by a train. When a train comes along, it shorts the circuit and signals its presence down the line. Signal cabinets are strategically positioned every few miles to relay these signals to stations ahead. Because they are frequently located in remote locations, the cabinets are often unguarded and vulnerable to sabotage by fire or even a sledgehammer. The loss of a signal cabinet along a critical section of line can shut down the railway in an entire region.

Shunt: A heavy-gauge wire is installed between the two rails. The resulting short circuit sends a "busy signal" to an oncoming locomotive that the track is occupied and will activate emergency braking procedures and result in a possible derailment.

Derailer: A Shavgulidze wedge bolts onto the tracks to derail the equipment as it rolls over it. These field-crafted derailers are painted a dark color and positioned to derail a train at a strategic point, such as in a tunnel, on a bridge, or at the bend of a curve, where repairing the damage will be difficult and time-consuming. Always place the derailer on the side of the track that you want the train to exit to cause maximum disruption.

Note: All information contained in this book is presented for educational purposes only. Many of the techniques are dangerous and should not be performed without training, supervision, and safety equipment, such as gloves, face mask, and eye protection. The authors, writers, editors, publisher, illustrator, and any other persons involved with this book are not liable for any damages, injuries, or legal actions that may arise from the use or misuse of any information contained herein. Always check the laws where you live and obey them. Don't do any harm and don't do any stupid stuff!

No. 069: Sabotage Railroads

CONOP: Railroad sabotage is an effective technique for disrupting the flow of men, material, and supplies to the battlefield.

COA1: Signal cabinets are frequently located in remote areas and unguarded. Attack them with fire (or napalm, see Skill 053), or a sledgehammer.

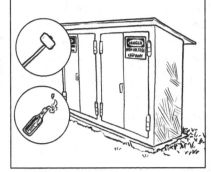

COA2: A shunt to short-circuit the signal can be improvised with a 5' length of heavy gauge wire and two metal clamps to attach to the rails.

COA3: Wedges or derailers can be fabricated or stolen from railroad yards and painted a dark color.

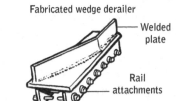

Fabricated wedge derailer
— Welded plate
Rail attachments

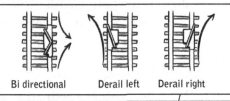

Bi directional   Derail left   Derail right

Stolen commercial derailer

BLUF: Stop the trains and win the war.

For informational purposes only,
exercise caution, prioritize safety, and obey all laws.

STEAL A TANK

Tank and armored vehicles may weigh as much as forty tons, cost millions of dollars, and are designed to outshoot, overpower, and overrun anyone or anything in their path.

Armored vehicles are often very complex, prone to breaking down, and require constant maintenance and fuel. While tanks are positioned at the vanguard of an invading army, the necessary fuel, spare parts, ammunition, and replacement crew members to keep them operating may be stranded in a convoy many miles away. When any armored vehicle can no longer move under its own power, because it is stuck in the mud, broken down, or out of fuel, it becomes a magnet for antitank missiles and is frequently abandoned by its disillusioned crew.

Fortunately for citizen soldiers, the typical armored vehicle has less antitheft protection than the riding lawn mower in your garage. Most armored vehicles can't be locked from the outside, and on tanks, access will always be available through the driver's hatch.

If you come across an abandoned tank or armored vehicle, do the following:

1. Check for booby traps.
2. If the treads or wheels are badly damaged, or it's stuck in the mud, some lightly armored vehicles can be towed using tractors.
3. A tank's primary control systems are located at the driver's position. The controls are unlocked and don't require a key!
4. Check the fuel gauge and see if the engine starts. If not, tow it away with tractors.
5. Alert nearby fire teams that the tank is now under your control. Display your flag prominently on the tank for friendly drones to spot.

No. 070: Steal a Tank

CONOP: Commandeer a tank or armored vehicle for operational use.

COA1: Check for battle damage that will prevent the tank or armored vehicle from moving.

COA2: Enter through the unlocked driver's hatch. It can't be locked from the outside.

ANATOMY OF A T-72

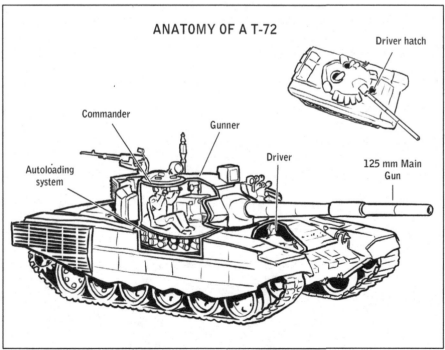

Commander

Gunner

Autoloading system

Driver

Driver hatch

125 mm Main Gun

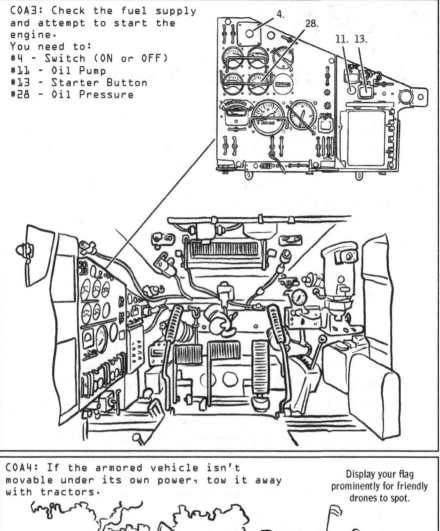

COA3: Check the fuel supply and attempt to start the engine.
You need to:
#4 - Switch (ON or OFF)
#11 - Oil Pump
#13 - Starter Button
#28 - Oil Pressure

4.
28.
11. 13.

COA4: If the armored vehicle isn't movable under its own power, tow it away with tractors.

Display your flag prominently for friendly drones to spot.

BLUF:
Armored vehicles are an intelligence bonanza for their communication gear, maps, machine guns, spare ammo, etc.

For informational purposes only,
exercise caution, prioritize safety, and obey all laws.

NO. 071

PROTECT AGAINST RPGS

The RPG (rocket-propelled grenade) is a reloadable shoulder-fired weapon that launches a rocket-assisted projectile equipped with fins for in-flight stability. It can use either HEAT (high-explosive antitank) warheads with shaped charges or HE (high-explosive) warheads for use against troops or unarmored vehicles or structures.

HEAT projectiles are most encountered and incorporate shaped charges to penetrate armor. When the warhead is detonated, a small core of molten metal forms and burns through the armor to cause destruction. However, causing the warhead to detonate prematurely, or not at all, can save your life!

Create a standoff with number 9 chain-link fencing that will electrically dud the grenade to prevent detonation. Though the nose cone of the round may pass through the screen, the electric firing signal from the nose fuse to the detonator will short out. The system isn't foolproof but works on approximately 50 percent of the rounds fired into it. Doubling the chain-link fencing and offsetting it slightly to decrease the openings between the links will increase your chances of surviving.

You can use this concept to mount a "see-through" and "shoot-through" screen in front of your bunker or around your vehicle! Ideally you want as much standoff distance as possible—at least eighteen to twenty-four inches around a vehicle and thirty-six inches or more in front of your bunker.

You'll need lengths of number 9 chain-link fencing and a way to stake it out in the ground or mount it in front of or along the sides of your vehicle. Portable dog kennels with panels of number 9 fencing may also be used as the basis for your protection.

No. 071: Protect Against RPGs

CONOP: RPGs are fearsome weapons and are carried by individual soldiers in conflicts around the world.

COA1: Acquire lengths of chain-link fencing, metal mounting rods, and small welding tools.

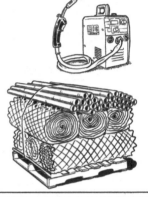

COA2: For vehicles create a metal frame to hold the length of chain link and mount it 18"-24" away from the vehicle. You can protect part or all the vehicle.

Protects driver, engine, & radiator

Protects cargo

COA3: Drive metal rods into the ground in front of your bunker and attach the chain link fence.

Electric firing signal

Explosive

Guide Fins

RPG-7VS

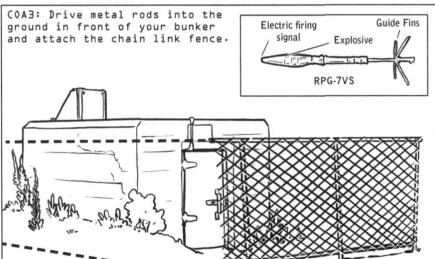

BLUF: Indirect fire is better than a direct hit.

3
SPECIAL
ACTIVITIES

SNIPER EVERYDAY CARRY

The selection of EDC sniper gear is always mission dependent and adjusted to the personal preferences of the shooter. What you'll need for a sniper overwatch is different from what you'll need for one-man reconnaissance or surveillance missions.

Essential sniper gear is sorted according into three lines.

First Line

Anything attached to your body, from boots to your uniform and the contents of your pockets.

- Your ballistic helmet, ghillie hat, or other headgear. A black beanie for nighttime use is always helpful to include in your pocket.
- Sunglasses are essential in maintaining your twenty/twenty vision.
- Camouflage clothing or a Ghillie suit must work in your operating environment. Muted dark colors are usually preferred unless operating in winter environments with snow.
- Include warm clothing as necessary. Sticking to darker muted colors is best.
- Avoid any pocket with a Velcro patch as being too noisy.
- A rigger's belt is ideal and can serve as a hoist or to rappel in an emergency.
- Gloves are essential, and ones that offer protection across the knuckles and greater sensitivity for the fingers are preferred.
- Footwear is a personal preference, but be sure to carry extra dry socks.
- Your clothing should always include a distinctive patch that indicates that you are wearing a uniform and subject to the rules of war.

No. 072: Sniper Every Day Carry

CONOP: Your EDC kit should include all the essential equipment needed to accomplish your mission and return.

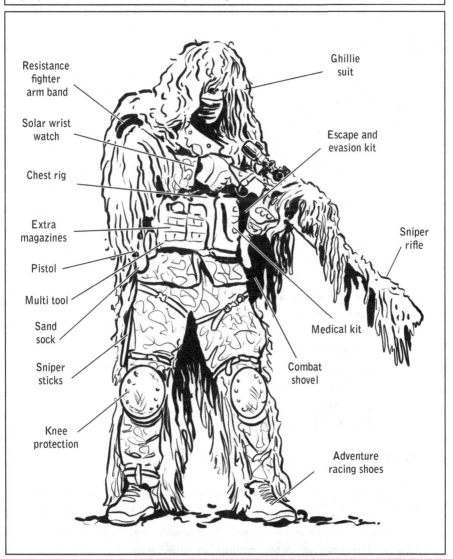

Resistance fighter arm band

Solar wrist watch

Chest rig

Extra magazines

Pistol

Multi tool

Sand sock

Sniper sticks

Knee protection

Ghillie suit

Escape and evasion kit

Sniper rifle

Medical kit

Combat shovel

Adventure racing shoes

BLUF: Travel Light, freeze at night.

For informational purposes only,
exercise caution, prioritize safety, and obey all laws.

- A small survival kit should include energy bars, water purification tablets, a pocketknife, signal mirror, camouflage paint, emergency compass, Bic-style lighter, etc. These should fill one of your cargo pockets.
- A small GPS system and map of the area are essential.

Second Line

Your fighting kit and anything attached to your belt or uniform, such as the following:

- Your sniper rifle.
- Sniper sticks and sand sock (see skill no. 077).
- Your chest rig will carry much of your kit and should be comfortable. Select one that will keep your hips free for ease of movement and hold lots of gear.
- Small combat shovel for creating mouseholes (see skill no. 027).
- An IR strobe for marking your position to your team.
- Night vision goggles if available and extra batteries.
- Canteen.
- Small flashlight and red filter.
- Extra ammunition for primary weapon and pistol.
- Binoculars, or spotting scope.
- Rangefinder.
- Assorted lengths of 550 paracord, Ranger Bands, and zip ties.
- Medical kit.
- Multitool.
- Communication gear.

Third Line

Any additional equipment that you might carry in a drag bag or backpack to meet your mission requirements and the length of time that you expect to be away from your supply source. This might include a camera, extra batteries, extra ammunition, water, etc.

HIGH-VALUE TARGETS

Identifying high-value targets (HVTs) on the battlefield in real time is a crucial task for a military force. HVTs are those individuals or assets that are of significant importance to the enemy force. Identifying and neutralizing these targets can have a significant impact on the outcome of a battle. Here are some strategies that can be used to identify HVTs on the battlefield in real time:

Firstly, intelligence gathering is a crucial aspect of identifying HVTs. It involves gathering information on enemy movements, tactics, and operations. Real-time intelligence can be obtained through various means, such as aerial surveillance, ground surveillance, and communication interception. Real-time intelligence can provide specific details on the location of HVTs, which can be used to target them.

Secondly, data analytics can also be used to identify HVTs in real time. This involves the use of algorithms that analyze data from various sources, such as social media, satellite imagery, and communication intercepts, to provide insights on the enemy's movements and activities. This data can be used to identify patterns and predict HVT locations.

Thirdly, battlefield sensors can also be used to identify HVTs in real time. These sensors can detect enemy movements, sound, and heat signatures, providing real-time information on the location of HVTs. This information can be relayed to the command center, allowing for swift action to be taken.

Lastly, trained soldiers can also identify HVTs in real time through their observations. This requires soldiers to have a keen eye and knowledge of enemy tactics and movements. Soldiers can identify HVTs by observing specific behaviors or equipment that is unique to HVTs.

In conclusion, identifying HVTs in real time requires a combination of tactics, including intelligence gathering, data analytics, battlefield sensors, and trained soldiers. Identifying HVTs accurately can provide a significant advantage in a battlefield situation, and it is essential to have reliable and efficient methods for identifying these targets.

No. 073: High-Value Targets

CONOP: Eliminating high value targets will disrupt enemy operations, demoralizes troops, and can paralyze an army.

COA1: Carefully study enemy uniforms and rank insignia. Target Majors and above.

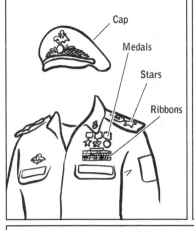

Cap

Medals

Stars

Ribbons

COA2: Target the oldest man standing next to vehicles with lots of antennas.

COA3: Target anyone holding a map and appearing to be giving orders.

COA4: Target a sniper or anyone in a Ghillie suit.

BLUF: Cut the head off a snake and the body will soon die.

For informational purposes only,
exercise caution, prioritize safety, and obey all laws.

NO. 074

SNIPER'S LAIR

While location is the primary consideration for a sniper, a site may sometimes be too good to use. For example, a lone water tower may provide a commanding view of the battlefield but not be good for sniping because it is too obvious and will be targeted because it has too few possible firing positions. Instead, a large building with many rooms and hundreds of potential loopholes and firing ports to shoot from and escape through provides greater anonymity. If the sniper position is in one of several similar buildings and shooting back and down at a steep angle toward the target, it becomes nearly impossible for reacting security forces to backtrack and identify the location.

Here are additional techniques to remain hidden:

1. While you must have a direct line of sight to the target, avoid corner rooms as they provide security forces with too many angles to scrutinize your sniper's lair.

2. Create an elevated firing position farther inside the room to make it more difficult to be spotted and to allow for a deeply angled shot. The more improbable the shooting angle, the greater your security.

3. Camouflage your position using a simple bedsheet that is the same color as the walls of the room. Drape it to cover both the rifle and shooter, and cut small openings for the scope and muzzle.

4. Hang a veil of thin mesh netting at a forty-five-degree angle in front of the rifle. The veil will make it difficult for an observer to see any details in the room and mask the muzzle flash.

5. Wear clothing that blends into the color of the room and your sheet.

No. 074: Sniper's Lair

CONOP: Hide in plain sight with the best vantage point.

COA1: Choose your location for anonymity and improbability.

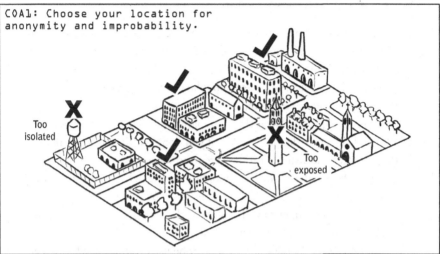

Too isolated

Too exposed

COA2: Position your elevated firing stand as far away from the window as possible.

COA4: Hang a section of thin mesh as a veil to mask the muzzle flash.

COA3: Shroud your firing position with a bedsheet to match the color of the interior walls.

BLUF: Concealment is important, but anonymity is priceless.

For informational purposes only, exercise caution, prioritize safety, and obey all laws.

NO. 075

LOOPHOLE

A loophole is a small opening in a wall or boarded-up window that allows a sniper to aim and shoot through while maintaining his cover and concealment. While a smaller loophole offers greater cover, it also limits the field of view. Conversely, larger loopholes offer a greater field of view but are more likely to be spotted by security forces.

In unique circumstances, the loophole could be as small as the size of a bullet hole in a boarded-up window if you don't require line of sight and both the target and firing position were fixed locations.

Using the smallest practical loophole conceals your position and significantly masks the sound of the gunshot, muzzle flash, and escaping gases. It allows the sniper to be invisible to thermal detection and lessens the need for him to relocate after each shot.

To find the smallest loophole that can be used to hit a fixed target at a known distance, do the following:

1. Establish your elevated firing position as far into the room as possible and adjust your scope for the known distance to the target.
2. With your rifle in a locked position and your crosshairs on the target, place a small dot on a piece of paper at the point it passes through the plane of the loophole.
3. Add a laser boresight to your rifle and mark a second dot on the paper at the point the laser impacts the plane of the loophole.
4. The distance between the two marks indicates the height of the smallest possible loophole that you can use to maintain line of sight to the target from your firing position.
5. Board up the window, leaving only the loophole.

No. 075: Loopholes

CONOP: Use the smallest loophole that allows a direct line-of-sight to the target, clear bullet path, and an adequate field of view.

COA1: Establish the firing position deep into the room and adjust your scope for the known target distance.

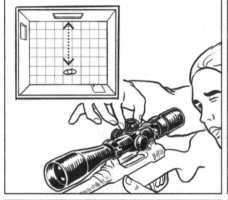

COA2: Put your cross hairs on the target and place a small dot on a piece of paper at the point it passes through the plane of the loophole.

COA3: With a laser bore sight mark a second dot on the paper at the point the laser impacts the plane of the loophole.

COA4: Measure the distance between the two marks to determine the smallest possible loophole. Board up the window and leave an opening for the small loophole.

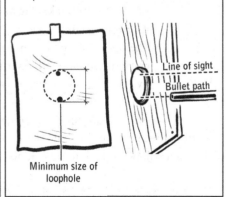

Line of sight

Bullet path

Minimum size of loophole

BLUF: For loopholes, smaller is always better.

NO. 076

ROOM SUPPRESSOR

A sniper's location is usually betrayed by sound and light. The sound of the gunshot generally reveals both the direction of the shot and the muzzle flash. Any dust kicked up by the escaping gasses from the barrel also serves to betray the firing location. Minimizing these factors makes it much harder to locate the sniper's position.

Citizen soldiers may have the time to convert an entire room into a sniper's hide and suppressor.

Here is what to do:

1. Select a room that appears deserted on an upper floor of a battle-damaged building. Nothing should visually make this room stand out.
2. Position your firing stand deep into the room and eight feet away from the window.
3. Create a platform to elevate your firing stand as needed to allow a direct line of sight to the target.
4. Suspend a series of six to eight or more old tires at the end of the barrel to form a tunnel through which the bullet will travel.
5. Before the shot, take care to water down the area at the end of the tunnel to minimize kicking up any dust.
6. The use of subsonic ammunition alone will eliminate the sonic crack of the shot and lower the sound by approximately twenty-five decibels. However, it also lowers the velocity and range.

The tires act as a suppressor to trap and collect the hot gasses escaping from the muzzle as the shot is fired. The sound of the shot will be muffled, and it will be difficult to determine the direction from which it was fired.

No. 076: Room Suppressor

CONOP: The use of a suppressor helps mask the sniper's location.

COA1: Select a room on the upper floor of a battle-damaged building.

Top floor ▶

COA2: Erect an elevated firing platform 8 feet into the room.

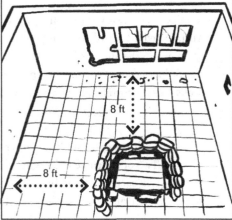

8 ft

8 ft

COA3: Use 6-8 suspended tires to form a tunnel for the bullet to travel.

BLUF: A single bullet in the right place can change the world.

For informational purposes only,
exercise caution, prioritize safety, and obey all laws.

SNIPER'S STICKS
AND SAND SOCK

A sniper requires a stable firing rest for accurate long-range shooting. An improvised set of shooting sticks and a sand sock can be important additions to the sniper's kit.

Sniper's sticks: The sniper can craft a portable tripod using three wood sticks (half inch in diameter and twenty-four to thirty inches long) and four feet of leather or paracord.

1. Lash the three sticks together toward the top using Prusik knots. Two of the three poles will become the shooting rest and the third will serve as the stabilizer.
2. The Prusik knots allow you to raise and lower the height of the shooting rest to match the firing location.
3. The sticks can be quickly bundled together and added to your pack or your belt as you move locations.

Sand sock: Use an old sock and some sand for a local play land to craft a multiposition portable firing rest. You'll need an old wool sock (calf- or boot-length are best) and some sand.

1. Fill the sock only halfway using sand or dirt. Consider using lightweight plastic beads to save weight.
2. With the sock halfway filled, twist the middle and sew it closed. Then pull the remainder of the sock back over itself and sew the top. Add a second sock as an additional cover for durability.

The sand sock can be used on the tripod or as a rest for other firing positions. It can also be used as a rear rest with the rifle resting on the tripod.

For informational purposes only,
exercise caution, prioritize safety, and obey all laws.

No. 077: Sniper Sticks and Sandsock

CONOP: A sniper requires a stable firing rest for accurate long-range shooting.

COA1: Craft a portable tripod using three wood sticks (1/2" in diameter and 24-30" long), and four feet of leather or paracord.

Prusik knot

COA2: Fill the sock only half-way full using sand or dirt and sew or tie the ends closed.

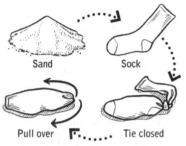

Sand   Sock

Pull over   Tie closed

COA3: Use the sniper's sticks alone, or with the sandsock better long-range accuracy.

Sandsock by itself

Handheld Tripod

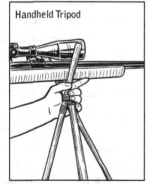

BLUF: Luck doesn't just happen, it's when preparation meets opportunity.

For informational purposes only,
exercise caution, prioritize safety, and obey all laws.

OIL FILTER SILENCER

On the battlefield, the biggest giveaways to locate the person shooting at you are flash and sound. If your weapon is quieter than the enemy's, and he can't see your muzzle flash or determine where the sound came from, you have the advantage. Using subsonic ammunition will also eliminate the tell-tale sonic crack.

Suppressors work by trapping all the supersonic hot gasses exiting the muzzle of the barrel as a bullet is fired. The speed of the gas is also slowed before exiting the muzzle and suppressor. This creates a lot of heat, but it also reduces the sound of the reported gunshot.

Citizen soldiers often don't have access to suppressed weapons, and a short-term alternative can be crafted from an oil filter and a machined adaptor for your rifle or pistol. When properly constructed, the sound from the gunshot will be significantly reduced by thirty to fifty decibels and the muzzle flash will be eliminated. For peak effectiveness, replace the oil filter every dozen shots.

A commercially available solvent trap and oil filter (or WIX fuel filter for diesels) consists of a perforated steel sleeve surrounded by a sound-dampening filler element and can be used as an alternate gun suppressor. The essential component you'll need to have machined is the adaptor that connects it to the barrel.

Warning: Making or owning a silencer is illegal in the US unless properly registered. Do not attempt to machine parts, drill holes, or otherwise do anything that could be construed as building an unregistered suppressor. All information contained in this book is presented for educational purposes only. Many of the techniques are dangerous and should not be performed without training, supervision, and safety equipment, such as gloves, face mask, and eye protection. The authors, writers, editors, publisher, illustrator, and any other persons involved with this book are not liable for any damages, injuries, or legal actions that may arise from the use or misuse of any information contained herein. Always check the laws where you live and obey them. Don't do any harm and don't do any stupid stuff!

No. 078: Oil Filter Suppressor

CONOP: Construct a disposable suppresor from an oil-filter.

COA1: Acquire the parts: Oil filter and machined adaptor.

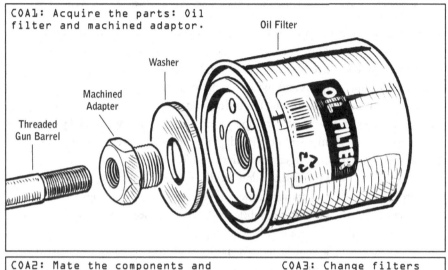

Oil Filter

Washer

Machined Adapter

Threaded Gun Barrel

COA2: Mate the components and fire a test round to create an opening at the end of the filter.

COA3: Change filters every dozen shots and carry spare filters you've already test fired in your kit.

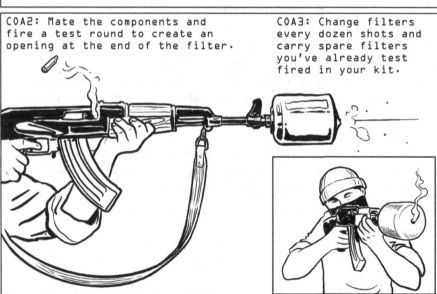

BLUF: Suppressing the sound and flash of a gunshot makes it difficult to pinpoint your location.

For informational purposes only, exercise caution, prioritize safety, and obey all laws.

VEHICLE SNIPER HIDE

Using a vehicle as a platform creates new opportunities for sniping as the vehicle itself provides a measure of cover and concealment. Almost all new vehicles allow the rear seat to be folded down and provide easy access to the trunk for weapons and hidden compartments.

A variety of off-the-shelf hunting and target rifles and associated ammunition are sufficient for sniper operations up to a few hundred yards. However, the vehicular hide is adaptable for specialized longer range weapons to take out targets more than a mile away.

Vehicles are modified to allow a full lie-down position for a sniper to fire through small openings in the rear of the vehicle. The firing port may be crude but still be effective, subtle, and well-disguised to pass unnoticed. Coupled with well-designed hidden compartments for the weapon and associated gear, a vehicle of this nature will be extremely difficult to differentiate from others that may travel through checkpoints.

A clear line of sight is required between the shooter and target, and effective vehicle hides permit shots to be taken at closer ranges.

Suppressed weapons are preferable, and the barrel should never protrude through the firing port. The body of the vehicle body serves to significantly mask muzzle flash and make it difficult to pinpoint the source of the gunshot.

A sniper team of two or more persons allows both the shooter and driver to concentrate on their respective responsibilities and not all aspects of an attack, thus increasing the probability of success and the ability to depart the area undetected.

No. 079: Vehicle Sniper Hide

CONOP: A vehicular sniper platform allows shots to be taken at closer ranges without attracting attention.

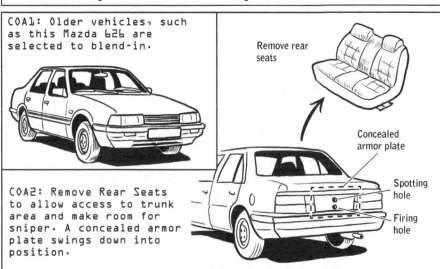

COA1: Older vehicles, such as this Mazda 626 are selected to blend-in.

Remove rear seats

COA2: Remove Rear Seats to allow access to trunk area and make room for sniper. A concealed armor plate swings down into position.

Concealed armor plate

Spotting hole

Firing hole

COA3: Position a Barrett .50 BMG M-82 inside. The shooter and driver must wear hearing protection and lower the armor plate after the shot.

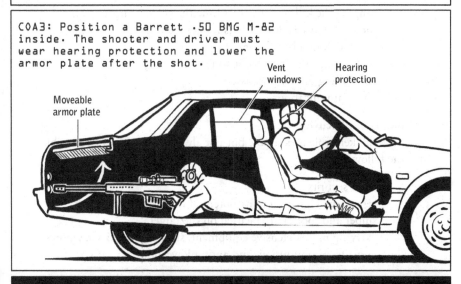

Vent windows

Hearing protection

Moveable armor plate

BLUF: The powerful overpressure from a single .50 caliber round can leave the shooter with a mild concussion.

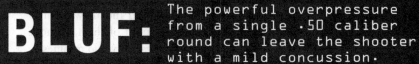

For informational purposes only,
exercise caution, prioritize safety, and obey all laws.

NO. 080

SNIPER TEAM

Though snipers can operate alone, teams involving at least two persons are more efficient and effective. Traditional two-man military sniper teams are composed of a shooter and a spotter. However, a third team member, the flanker, is desirable to provide the team with enhanced security.

Shooter

The shooter is the team leader and responsible for the following:

- the sniper rifle and ammunition
- selecting the sniper hide and making the decision to shoot
- route selection (in, out, and escape)

Spotter

The spotter is also the second shooter and responsible for the following:

- working with the sniper to observe and engage the enemy
- ranging the kill zone to determine the correct target distance
- monitoring variables, such as ranges, elevation, wind speed, and wind direction before the shot
- monitoring results and adjusting if necessary
- controlling fire support assets
- all communications

Flanker/Rear Security

The flanker's role is desirable but not always filled. He is responsible for the following:

- team security
- remaining vigilant for any potential threat to the team while the sniper and spotter are focused on the target
- carrying more defensive equipment, such as M18A1 Claymores, grenades, ammunition, and antitank weaponry

Knowing that the flanker is focused on the team's security can give both the sniper and the spotter greater peace of mind and allow them to focus more on their own tasks, and the area in front of them, without having to worry about checking their surroundings every two minutes.

198

No. 080: Sniper Team

CONOP: Three-man sniper teams are more efficient and effective.

COA1: The Shooter is responsible for his rifle, selecting the hide, and making the shot.

Rear Security

Spotter

Shooter

COA2: The Spotter is responsible for 'ranging the kill zone' to determine the correct target distance.

Range-finding binoculars

COA3: The Rear Security is responsible for any potential threats to the team while the sniper and spotter are focused on the target.

Assault rifle + grenade launcher

Anti-tank weaponry

Claymores

BLUF: A sniper can be your best friend, or your worst enemy.

For informational purposes only,
exercise caution, prioritize safety, and obey all laws.

NO. 081

SHOOT TO WOUND, NOT KILL

War is bloody, messy, and horrid beyond description. In the simplest terms, wars are won simply by achieving goals with minimal loss to your own forces. If an attacking force is closing in on your position, you should, of course, always shoot to kill. However, body counts alone don't determine victory, and in some special circumstances, it may be better to wound an attacker than kill him.

Even though attackers often abandon their dead comrades on the battlefield, care is still taken to retrieve and care for their wounded if only to maintain morale. It requires four attackers to carry a wounded comrade off the battlefield and between two and six people plus logistics to treat the wounds and transport them to a hospital for additional care. The overall time, resources, and expertise expended on a wounded soldier is many times greater than for a dead one.

In circumstances where an attacking force is crossing an open area in front of your position, shooting to wound may be wise. Snipers can readily place shots accurately over intermediate distances to target vulnerabilities in an adversary's body armor. As such, they can also elect to target a vulnerable part of his body beneath the lower body armor: the balls. A shot there will likely ricochet about the pelvic girdle and do terrible damage. A shot in the groin area will likely prove fatal, but death won't come quickly. When his comrades come to retrieve him, you should then shoot to kill. Seeing comrades dying in a wasted rescue effort is an effective way to demoralize an already unmotivated force invading your country.

No. 081: Shoot to Wound, not Kill

CONOP: Overwhelm enemy forces with the care necessary for the screaming injured instead of the dead who remain silent.

COA1: Target an attacker with a shot aimed between the knees and bellybutton, and lure other to come to his rescue.

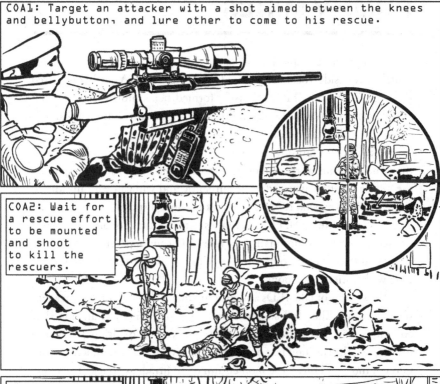

COA2: Wait for a rescue effort to be mounted and shoot to kill the rescuers.

COA3: Repeat the process as more wounded are on the battlefield awaiting rescue.

BLUF: Casualties suck up more time, effort, and resources than dead bodies.

FAKE IEDS AND DUMMY MINES

IEDs (improvised explosive devices) can be concealed in buildings, vehicles, roadside trash, or planted in the ground. A well-configured IED containing an EFP (explosively formed penetrator) can knock out even heavily armored vehicles and become a constant source of fear and apprehension for their crew.

Fake IEDs or dummy mines are intended to look like and to give off the same signature as the real devices to deceive the enemy. Once spotted, the device must be assumed to be authentic and will cause an invader to waste time and expend EOD (explosive ordnance disposal) assets to reduce or defuse the threat. All of which takes valuable time, effort, and drains limited resources. Additionally, if a fake IED causes an entire column or convoy to stop, they become vulnerable to mobile fire teams (see skill no. 052) with antitank weapons.

The success of fake IEDs and dummy mines depends on the invader's state of mind. The bluff succeeds best when the enemy is already IED conscious and has suffered the consequences of roadside IEDs and minefields. The constant fear of unseen explosive devices can quickly evolve into paranoia and break the momentum of an invader's attack. Therefore, fake IEDs and mines are normally employed only in conjunction with some real devices and are seldom used alone.

For the threat to be credible, the fake devices must completely replicate their live counterparts in every detail and be emplaced in the same manner. Every aspect of the fakes must support the deception story.

No. 082: Dummy Mines

CONOP: Deceive and delay the enemy with dummy land mines.

COA1: Acquire Supplies:

Duct Tape

Digital watch

Black spray paint

Metal trash can lid

COA2: Remove Handle and spray paint the Trash Can lid flat black.

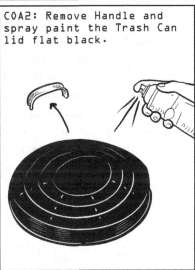

COA3: Tape the digital watch to the underside of the trash can lid.

COA4: Fake mines will trip junction detectors, confuse the enemy, and cause delays for mine removal operations.

BLUF: There is nothing more deceptive than the obvious.

For informational purposes only,
exercise caution, prioritize safety, and obey all laws.

CALTROPS

Tire spikes (caltrops) are area denial weapons that were first used centuries ago to disable camels (and later horses) during a pursuit. They work just as effectively to puncture pneumatic tires on vehicles and airplanes.

No matter how the tire spike is thrown, it always lands with one of its four spikes in a vertical, upright position. Because the spikes are hollow, when the tire is punctured, the air rushes out within seconds and the tire goes flat. Spikes that are painted with black primer are especially effective and difficult to spot at night when scattered on enemy roads and airfields.

Tire spikes may be thrown from a moving vehicle to stop pursuers or distributed across a roadway as a spike strip to stop reinforcements.

Make your own four-inch diameter tire spikes using three-eighth-inch, hollow, heavy, steel tubes.

1. Using a torch to heat and bend a hollow tube at a ninety-degree angle every two inches.
2. Use a portable bandsaw to cut the pieces apart every four inches. Make your cut on an angle so that every end is sharpened.
3. Weld the two spikes together at right-angles so that no matter how they are thrown, they land with a pointed spike in the vertical position.
4. Paint both sides with nonreflective black or brown primer as camouflage.

To make a mobile spike strip, use chain-link to string caltrops every six inches. If you are protecting a fifteen-foot roadway, you'll need thirty caltrops.

No. 083: Caltrops

CONOP: No matter how they are thrown, caltrops land with a pointed spike upward and will destroy the tires of pursuing vehicles.

COA1: Acquire a length of 3/8" hollow heavy steel tubes, welding tools, vice, and a handsaw.

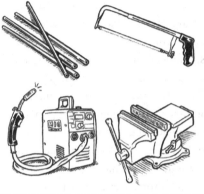

COA2: Using a torch to heat and bend a hollow tube at a 90 degree angle every 2 inches.

COA3: Weld the two spikes together at right-angles so that no matter how they are thrown, they land with a pointed spike in the vertical position.

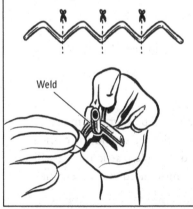

Weld

COA4: Paint both sides with non-reflective black or brown primer as camouflage.

BLUF: Stop the enemy in their tracks.

For informational purposes only,
exercise caution, prioritize safety, and obey all laws.

SABOTAGE COMBUSTION ENGINES

Disrupting the adversary's transportation and logistics systems will delay the distribution of munitions, tanks, fuel, spare parts, medicine, and soldiers. Ideally the sabotage device must be easily concealed on a person, rapid to deploy, effective in small quantities, and leave no clue as to its origin. Disabling a vehicle away from its base of operations is preferred as it diverts additional resources for its recovery and shields the saboteur from suspicion.

Field testing determined that common combustion engine attacks using gasoline contaminants (sugar, styrene, etc.) were unsuccessful. Success was eventually achieved using a special oil contaminant to permanently disable the combustion engine by damaging its pistons, bearings, and cylinder block. Once the contaminant circulates in the oil supply, it fuses and welds the moving parts of the engine. Total destruction of the engine will occur in approximately half an hour.

The contaminant can be used against other combustion engines, including those found on piston aircraft, tanks, and in factories.

After an exhaustive study, the most effective oil contaminant ingredients are these:

- sixty-eight parts aluminum-magnesium (Special All-Mag powder),
- six parts dried cork (ground)
- eight parts dry resin (ground)

The ingredients must be finely ground into a powder and mixed to effectively circulate throughout the engine's lubrication system and carried in a small plastic bottle. Adding two feet of flexible plastic tubing will allow the contents of the bottle to be rapidly introduced into the engine's oil lubrication system.

Note: In an emergency, smashing the battery and cutting all hoses and wiring in the engine compartment will take the vehicle out of action for days or weeks.

No. 084: Combustion Engine Sabotage

CONOP: Disrupting the adversary's transportation and logistics systems will delay the distribution of war supplies.

COA1: Gather the supplies

Aluminum-magnesium

Dry resin

Cork

COA2: Compound and mix carefully. It should be finely ground, but not too fine.

COA3: Mix the solution into a small one-ounce bottle with a long plastic tube attached.

1 oz Bottle w/ Tube

COA4: Insert into the oil supply filler for destruction.

Automobile

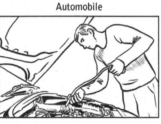

Heavy Machinery

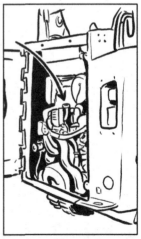

Motorcycle

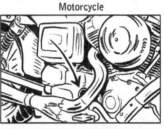

BLUF: Amateurs focus on strategy. Saboteurs target logistics.

Note: All information contained in this book is presented for educational and informational purposes only. Many of the techniques are dangerous and should not be performed without training, proper supervision, and safety equipment, such as gloves, face mask, and eye protection. The authors, writers, editors, publisher, illustrator, and any other persons involved with this book are not liable for any damages, injuries, or legal actions that may arise from the use or misuse of any information contained herein. Always check the laws where you live and obey them. Don't do any harm and don't do any stupid stuff!

DELAYED REACTION INCENDIARY FIRE

The most important consideration in planning and carrying out an act of sabotage is using a time delay to allow the saboteur to escape the area before the fire begins. Capsule H provides that delayed capability.

Capsules H are small plastic capsules containing a mixture of powdered potassium chlorate and powdered sugar weighted with buckshot. The capsules are constructed in two separate thicknesses of plastic.

Capsule H causes a fire to be ignited by chemical reaction after a time delay. The Capsule H contains only part of the necessary chemicals for the fire. The other necessary ingredient is sulfuric acid, which will take about two hours to eat through the plastic capsules and ignite the powder. The citizen soldier saboteur will find this acid in his own or enemy sources of supply. It may also be found in regular storage batteries if not available elsewhere.

The best method of improving this highly effective incendiary is to place a small amount of liquid acid in a medium-size bottle, drop in two or more Capsules H, and fill the bottle with gasoline or other in flammable liquid, such as half gas and half oil. Inverting the bottle so that the acid in capsules is concentrated in the neck ensures efficiency. The acid will eat through the plastic capsules in approximately two hours and ignite the powders with a brief hot flame.

The bursting bottle of dispersed flaming gasoline should be placed where it can quickly spread to any highly combustible material.

Note: All information contained in this book is presented for educational and informational purposes only. Many of the techniques are dangerous and should not be performed without training, proper supervision, and safety equipment, such as gloves, face mask, and eye protection. The authors, writers, editors, publisher, illustrator, and any other persons involved with this book are not liable for any damages, injuries, or legal actions that may arise from the use or misuse of any information contained herein. Always check the laws where you live and obey them. Don't do any harm and don't do any stupid stuff!

No. 085: Delayed Incendiary Device

CONOP: A time-delay allows the saboteur to safely escape the area before the fire.

COA1: Gather your supplies:

 Gasoline

 Glass bottle

 Sulfuric acid

 Powdered sugar

 Buck shot

 Medicine capsules

Potassium chlorate

COA2: Create the Capsules H and store them in a tightly sealed jar.

Buck Shot
Powdered sugar
Potassium chlorate
Capsule H

COA3: Select a target where the fire will cause the greatest damage to materials and equipment.

Activated Incendiary

Gasoline/Sulfuric acid mixture

Capsule H

BLUF: The further away you can be from the fire, the better.

For informational purposes only,
exercise caution, prioritize safety, and obey all laws.

NO. 086

SABOTAGE BRIDGES

Bridges are essential for the transportation of troops, vehicles, equipment, and supplies. Without bridges armies can't cross rivers or gorges and soldiers run out of bullets.

The five main styles of bridges are beam, arch, truss, cantilever, and suspension. Explosives are used to weaken steel plates, girders, cables, or other key structural elements so that the unsupported weight of the bridge will cause it to self-destruct.

Beam: The oldest and simplest design where flat beams are supported by abutments on the banks and sometimes by piers in the middle. Charges should be placed in the middle of the flat beam between supports.

Arch: One of the oldest bridge designs. Charges should be placed on both sides of the center point of the roadway.

Truss: A diagonal mesh of reinforcing triangles above the bridge that distribute forces across the entire bridge structure. Charges should be placed at the corners of the triangle reinforcements.

Cantilever: Reinforcing triangles placed beneath the bridge to distribute forces across the structure. Charges should be placed at the corners of the triangle reinforcements.

Suspension: Spreading ropes or cables from the vertical shafts to hold the weight of bridge deck and traffic. Charges should be placed on the top and bottom of the vertical shafts to which the ropes and cables are attached.

Large charges (forty-four to sixty-six pounds/twenty to thirty kilograms) of conventional explosives placed and tamped down at vulnerable points on the bridge should be detonated simultaneously for the greatest effect. Shaped charges will create greater damage with smaller amounts of plastic explosives.

No. 086: Sabotage Bridges

CONOP: Attack the enemy's ability to wage war by sabotaging bridges on key logistic routes at their most vulnerable points.

COA 1: Truss Bridge

Place at Triangular Reinforcements.

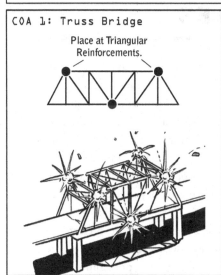

COA 2: Suspension Bridge

Place on the top and bottom of the vertical shafts.

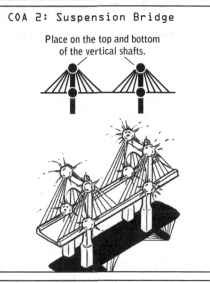

COA 3: Arch Bridge

Place at both sides of center point.

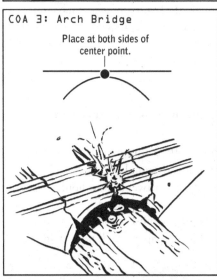

COA 4: Beam Bridge

Place in the middle of the flat beam between supports.

BLUF: Bridges are high priority targets for sabotage.

For informational purposes only,
exercise caution, prioritize safety, and obey all laws.

NO. 087

FUSES FOR EXPLOSIVES AND FLAMMABLES

Note: All information contained in this book is presented for educational and informational purposes only. Many of the techniques are dangerous and should not be performed without training, proper supervision, and safety equipment, such as gloves, face mask, and eye protection. The authors, writers, editors, publisher, illustrator, and any other persons involved with this book are not liable for any damages, injuries, or legal actions that may arise from the use or misuse of any information contained herein. Always check the laws where you live and obey them. Don't do any harm and don't do any stupid stuff!

Simple fuses burn at a slow and steady rate and are preferred for igniting explosive charges. Here's how to improvise a fuse in an emergency.

You'll need a long shoelace (or cotton yarn), potassium nitrate (saltpeter), sugar, two bowls, and some water. The key ingredient, potassium nitrate (KNO_3), is marketed commercially as "stump remover" or may be sourced as fertilizer.

For Igniting Explosives

1. Take a length of shoelace (or yarn) and soak it in water for a few seconds.
2. Place it inside a container with a 50/50 mixture of potassium nitrate (saltpeter) and sugar until it is thoroughly coated.
3. Stretch the shoelace out and let it dry for twenty-four hours.

Cut the fuse to length for use with smoke bombs (see skill no. 096).

For igniting a pile of flammable rubbish or paper, you'll need string, grease, and gunpowder.

1. Soak one end of a piece of string in grease.
2. Rub a generous pinch of gunpowder over one inch of string at the end.

No. 087: Fuses for Explosives and Flammables

CONOP: Use a slow-burning fuse to ignite the incendiary after you are safely away before the fire.

COA1: You'll need a long shoelace or yarn, potassium nitrate (salt peter), sugar, bowls, and some water.

COA2: Take a length of shoelace (or yarn) and soak it in water for a few seconds.

COA3: Place it inside a container with a 50/50 mixture of potassium nitrate (salt peter) and sugar until it is thoroughly coated.

COA4: Stretch the shoelace out and let it dry for 24 hours.

BLUF: Fuses provide time, and time provides options.

For informational purposes only,
exercise caution, prioritize safety, and obey all laws.

Once the clean end of the string is lit, it will burn slowly without a flame (like a cigarette burns) until it reaches the grease and gunpowder. It will then flare up suddenly to ignite the flammables. You can also substitute matchheads instead of the grease and powder. The advantage of this type of fuse is that string burns at a certain speed. You can time your fire by the length and thickness of the string you choose.

SABOTAGE AN ENGINE COMPARTMENT

Creating a fire in an engine compartment will fry the vehicle's essential wiring, electrical components, rubber seals, and hoses and take it out of action indefinitely. What's needed for the saboteur, however, is a means of delaying the ignition of the fire until he can flee the area.

What you'll need are chlorine tablets from a pool supply or water treatment plant, sugar, aluminum filings from an old window screen, coffee can, cheesecloth or coffee filter paper, string, and your multitool.

1. Place a two-inch bed of a 50/50 mix of sugar and aluminum filings in the bottom of the coffee can.
2. Place the chlorine tablet on top of the mixture.
3. Cover the can with cheesecloth or coffee filter paper and tie in place with string.

The saboteur will access the vehicle's engine compartment and use the multitool to make a small saw cut in one of the metal lines leading into the brake fluid reservoir to create a leak. Position the coffee can beneath the reservoir to catch the drip.

As the cheesecloth (or filter paper) slowly becomes saturated with brake fluid, it will eventually drip down into the can and react with the chlorine. Granular chlorine (calcium hypochlorite) and brake fluid (polyethylene glycol) react violently when mixed, producing a fierce fireball. The presence of the sugar and aluminum filings will create the intense heat needed to melt the engine's rubber and electrical components.

Note: All information contained in this book is presented for educational and informational purposes only. Many of the techniques are dangerous and should not be performed without training, proper supervision, and safety equipment, such as gloves, face mask, and eye protection. The authors, writers, editors, publisher, illustrator, and any other persons involved with this book are not liable for any damages, injuries, or legal actions that may arise from the use or misuse of any information contained herein. Always check the laws where you live and obey them. Don't do any harm and don't do any stupid stuff!

No. 088: Fire in a Can

CONOP: Every enemy vehicle taken out of action hurts their war effort.

COA1: Acquire chlorine tablets, sugar, aluminum filings, coffee can, heesecloth or coffee filter paper, string, and multitool.

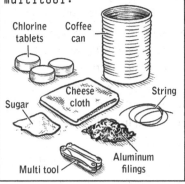

Chlorine tablets
Coffee can
Cheese cloth
String
Sugar
Multi tool
Aluminum filings

COA2: Place a 2" bed of a 50/50 mix of sugar and aluminum filings in the bottom of the coffee can.

COA3: Place the chlorine tablets on top of the mixture.

Empty coffee can

Chlorine tablets

50/50 mix of aluminum filings and sugar

COA4: Cover the can with cheesecloth or coffee filter paper and tie in place with string.

Cheese cloth

COA5: Make a small cut into the metal brake-reservoir line and place the covered can beneath it to catch the drips.

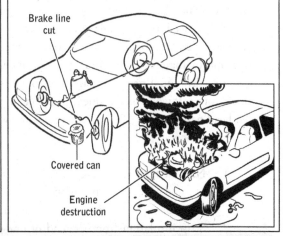

Brake line cut

Covered can

Engine destruction

BLUF: Burn it down.

PRESSURE PLATE SWITCH

A pressure plate switch is a type of switch that is activated when a physical force is applied to the surface of the switch. It works in a similar way to a button, but instead of being pushed, it is activated by the weight or pressure of an object. This makes it useful for a variety of applications, such as in doorbells, alarms, and security systems. When the switch is pressed, it completes an electrical circuit and allows current to flow. Pressure plate switches are often used in situations where it is not practical to use a traditional button or switch because they can be activated without needing much force or motor control. They are available in a range of sizes and designs to suit different applications and can be used in both commercial and industrial settings.

Make a pressure-sensitive switch to initiate an emplaced explosive and destroy an armored vehicle.

The switch is placed in a hole in the path of expected armored vehicle traffic and covered with a thin layer of dirt or other camouflaging material. When the armored vehicle passes over the switch, its extra weight causes the two metal plates to make contact and close the firing circuit.

You'll need two flexible metal sheets or flattened tin cans, one approximately ten inches (twenty-five centimeters) square and a second one approximately ten inches by eight inches (twenty centimeters). Additionally, you'll need a square piece of wood ten inches by one inch thick, four soft wood blocks one inch by one inch by a quarter inch, eight flat head nails, one inch long, and connecting wires.

Here's how:

1. Nail the ten-inch by eight-inch metal sheet to the ten-inch piece of wood so that one inch of wood shows on each side of the metal. Leave one nail sticking up a quarter inch.
2. Strip insulation from the end of one connecting wire, wrap it around the nail, and drive it in.
3. Place the four wood blocks on the corners of the wood base.

No. 089: Pressure Plate Switch

CONOP: Enemy forces usually deploy armored vehicles at the vanguard of their attacks.

COA1: Acquire:

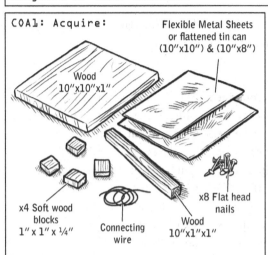

Wood 10"x10"x1"

Flexible Metal Sheets or flattened tin can (10"x10") & (10"x8")

x4 Soft wood blocks 1" x 1" x ¼"

Connecting wire

Wood 10"x1"x1"

x8 Flat head nails

COA2: Nail the 10" x 8" metal sheet to the 10" piece of wood so that 1" of wood shows on each side of the metal. Leave one nail sticking up ¼ inch.

COA3: Strip insulation from the end of one connecting wire and wrap it around the nail.

COA4: Place the four wood blocks on the corners of the wood base.

COA5: Place the 10" square flexible metal sheet so that it rests on the four blocks.

COA6: Drive the nails through the metal sheet and to fasten the blocks. A second connecting wire is attached to one of the nails as in step 2.

Wrap adhesive tape around base to keep out rocks and debris.

When an armored vehicle passes over the switch, the metal plates make contact and close the circuit to activate the explosive charge.

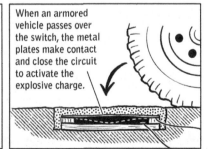

BLUF: Place obstacles to channel armored vehicle traffic over the pressure-plate switch.

For informational purposes only, exercise caution, prioritize safety, and obey all laws.

4. Place the ten-inch square flexible metal sheet so that it rests on the four blocks.
5. Drive the nails through the metal sheet and to fasten the blocks. A second connecting wire is attached to one of the nails as in step two.
6. Wrap adhesive tape around the edges of the plate and wood base to assure that no dirt or other foreign matter will get between the plates.

Note: All information contained in this book is presented for educational and informational purposes only. Many of the techniques are dangerous and should not be performed without training, proper supervision, and safety equipment, such as gloves, face mask, and eye protection. The authors, writers, editors, publisher, illustrator, and any other persons involved with this book are not liable for any damages, injuries, or legal actions that may arise from the use or misuse of any information contained herein. Always check the laws where you live and obey them. Don't do any harm and don't do any stupid stuff!

NO. 090

MOUSETRAP SWITCH

Note: All information contained in this book is presented for educational and informational purposes only. Many of the techniques are dangerous and should not be performed without training, proper supervision, and safety equipment, such as gloves, face mask, and eye protection. The authors, writers, editors, publisher, illustrator, and any other persons involved with this book are not liable for any damages, injuries, or legal actions that may arise from the use or misuse of any information contained herein. Always check the laws where you live and obey them. Don't do any harm and don't do any stupid stuff!

A common mousetrap can be used to make a circuit closing switch for electrically initiated explosives, mines, and booby traps.

The switch can be used in several ways. One typical method is inside a box or gift-wrapped package. The switch, explosive, and battery are placed inside a box. The spring-loaded striker is held back by the lid of the box, and when the box is opened, the circuit is closed and then detonates the explosive.

The mousetrap can also be used as a pressure-release switch when placed beneath a heavier object that will hold back the spring-loaded striker. The object might even be a laptop or other high-value electronic item. When the object is lifted, the pressure is released and the completed firing circuit detonates the explosive.

You'll need a common mousetrap and a hacksaw or file.

Here's how:

1. Remove the triple lever from the mousetrap using a hacksaw or file. Also remove the staple and holding wire.
2. Retract the striker of the mousetrap and attach the crypt lever across the end of the wood base using the staple with which the holding wire was attached.
3. Strip one inch (2.5 centimeters) of insulation from the ends of two connecting wires.
4. Wrap one wire tightly around the spring-loaded striker of the mousetrap.
5. Wrap the second wire around some part of the trip lever or piece of metal.

No. 090: Mousetrap Switch

CONOP: Invaders are less likely to loot and pillage if they fear boob-traps.

COA1: Acquire a common mousetrap and a hacksaw or file.

COA2: Remove the triple lever from the mouse trap using a hacksaw or file. Also remove the staple and holding wire.

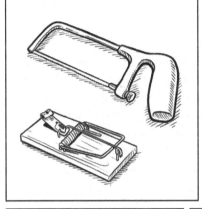

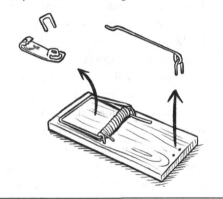

COA3: Retract the striker of the mouse trap and attach the crypt lever across the end of the wood base using the staple with which the holding wire was attached.

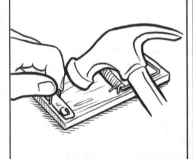

COA4: Strip 1" (2 ½ cm) of insulation from the ends of two connecting wires and wrap one wire tightly around the spring-loaded striker of the mousetrap.

COA5: Wrap the second wire around some part of the trip lever or piece of metal.

COA6: By concealing the mousetrap switch underneath a package, lifting the package will trigger an explosion.

BLUF: Looters deserve a special surprise when they steal!

For informational purposes only,
exercise caution, prioritize safety, and obey all laws.

NO. 091

CLOTHESPIN TIME-DELAY SWITCH

Note: All information contained in this book is presented for educational and informational purposes only. Many of the techniques are dangerous and should not be performed without training, proper supervision, and safety equipment, such as gloves, face mask, and eye protection. The authors, writers, editors, publisher, illustrator, and any other persons involved with this book are not liable for any damages, injuries, or legal actions that may arise from the use or misuse of any information contained herein. Always check the laws where you live and obey them. Don't do any harm and don't do any stupid stuff!

A three- to five-minute time-delay switch can be made from a clothespin, cigarette, solid or stranded copper wire, some fine string, and a knife. The system can be used to initiate explosive charges, mines, and booby traps.

Here how:

1. Strip about four inches (ten centimeters) of insulation from the ends of two copper wires. Scrape copper wires with pocketknife until metal is shiny.
2. Cut shallow notches in the ends of the clothespin one-eighth inch from the end to hold the string.
3. Wind one scraped wire tightly on one jaw of the clothespin and the other wire on the other jaw so that the wires will be in contact when closed.
4. The length of cigarette used will correspond to the desire delay time. Make a hole in the cigarette (not the filter) at this point using wire or a pin.
5. Thread string through hole and cigarette.
6. Tie string around rear of clothespin, one eighth of an inch or less, and suspend the entire system vertically with the cigarette tip down. Light tip of cigarette. The switch will close, and initiation will occur with the cigarette burns up to and through the string. The clothespin may be notched to hold the string in place and keep the jaws open.

No. 091: Clothespin Time-delay Switch

CONOP: A time delay switch allows time for you to be as far away as possible when the explosion occurs.

COA1: Acquire a clothespin, cigarette, solid or stranded copper wire, some fine string, and a knife.

COA2: Strip about 4 inches (10 cm) of insulation from the ends of two copper wires. Scrape copper wires with pocketknife until metal is shiny.

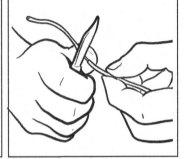

COA3: Wind one scraped wire tightly on one jaw of the clothespin, and the other wire on the other jaw so that the wires will be in contact when closed.

COA4: The length of cigarette used will correspond to the desire delay time. Make a hole in the cigarette at this point using wire or a pin.

COA5: Thread string through hole and cigarette.

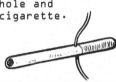

COA6: Tie string around clothes pin, and suspend the entire system vertically with the cigarette tip down. Light cigarette. The switch will close, and initiation will occur when the cigarette burns through the string.

Closed circuit

For informational purposes only,
exercise caution, prioritize safety, and obey all laws.

How to use:

Suspend the entire system vertically with the cigarette tip down. The switch will close, and initiation will occur with the cigarette burns up to and through the string.

Note: Delay time may be adjusted by varying the burning length of the cigarette. Burning rate in still air is approximately seven minutes per inch. However, this rate varies with the environment and brand of cigarettes. Test in advance for accuracy.

HASTY CELL PHONE KILLER

Your cell phone can get you killed during wartime. Adversarial technical capabilities allow your location to be tracked and the geographical coordinates sent to weapons systems to kill you.

An improvised Faraday cage (see skill no. 014) is an effective solution, but it's big and bulky and not practical for your EDC kit. What's needed is an inexpensive radio frequency blocking bag that will prevent your phone from sending or receiving any signals and be small enough to carry with you.

To make one, you'll two foil potato chip (or similar foil) bags, a small plastic sandwich bag, and some tape.

1. Turn your phone off and seal it inside a plastic sandwich bag.
2. Take an empty foil chip bag, press flat, and insert the bagged phone.
3. Place the foil bag flat on a counter and remove all air. Fold each of the two open corners at forty-five degrees (hospital corner).
4. Fold the top at half-inch increments until you are halfway down the bag. Then seal and tape the folded portion to the bag. It should now be airtight and RF tight.
5. Repeat the process after inserting bag number 1 into bag number 2.
6. Carry the completed bag close to your body in an inside chest pocket to further attenuate any signal.

Note: Be certain that the phone is turned off! Otherwise, your cell phone will continuously increase the strength of its signal to contact the closest cell tower or loitering snooper drone and betray your location.

No. 092: Hasty Dirty Cell Phone Killer

CONOP: Adversaries can remotely use your cell phone signal to track your location and target you on the battlefield.

COA1: Acquire two foil potato chip (or similar) bags, a small plastic sandwich bag and some tape.

COA2: Turn your phone off and seal it inside a plastic sandwich style bag.

COA3: Place the plastic bag and phone inside the first sandwich bag.

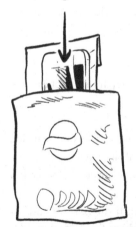

COA4: Fold and tape the first bag closed, then place in second sandwich bag and tape shut.

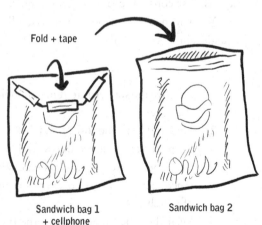

Fold + tape

Sandwich bag 1 + cellphone

Sandwich bag 2

BLUF: Silence may be golden, but cell phone anonymity can save your life!

For informational purposes only, exercise caution, prioritize safety, and obey all laws.

MATCHBOOK IGNITER

Note: All information contained in this book is presented for educational and informational purposes only. Many of the techniques are dangerous and should not be performed without training, proper supervision, and safety equipment, such as gloves, face mask, and eye protection. The authors, writers, editors, publisher, illustrator, and any other persons involved with this book are not liable for any damages, injuries, or legal actions that may arise from the use or misuse of any information contained herein. Always check the laws where you live and obey them. Don't do any harm and don't do any stupid stuff!

A simple but reliable match-striker can be crafted from a standard paper book of matches and used to ignite a Molotov cocktail (see skill no. 053). In operational use, the "cover end tab" of the igniter is pulled upward sharply and quickly to light the matches before the bottle is thrown.

The matchbook igniter can also be used by itself to ignite flammable liquids, fuse cords, and similar items requiring hot ignition.

You will need paper book matches, adhesive or friction tape, and a straight pin or small nail.

Here's how:

1. Remove the staple(s) from matchbook and separate matches from the cover.
2. Fold and tape one row of matches.
3. Shape the cover into a tube with the striking surface on the inside and tape. Make sure the folded cover will fit tightly around the taped matches. Leave cover open at the opposite end for insertion of matches.
4. Push the taped matches into the tube until the bottom ends of the matches are exposed approximately three-fourths of an inch (two centimeters).

No. 093: Matchbook Igniter

CONOP: Flammable liquids are useless without a reliable means to spark ignition.

COA1: Acquire paper book matches, adhesive or friction tape, and a straight pin or small nail.

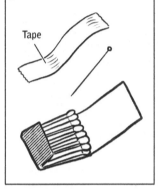

Tape

COA2: Remove the staple(s) from matchbook and separate matches from the cover.

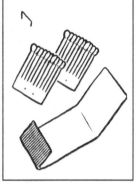

COA3: Fold and tape one row of matches.

Tape

COA4: Shape the cover into a tube with the striking surface on the inside and tape.

COA5: Push the taped matches into the tube until the bottom ends of the matches are exposed approximately 3/4".

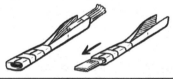

COA6: Flatten and fold the open the end of the tube so that it laps over about 1 inch (2 ½ cm); tape in place.

Fold & tape

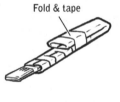

COA7: Tape the "match end tab" of the igniter to the neck of the Molotov Cocktail. Pull to ignite matches.

5. Flatten and fold the open the end of the tube so that it laps over about one inch (2.5 centimeters); tape in place.

6. Tape the "match end tab" of the igniter to the neck of the Molotov cocktail.

Caution: Store matches and completed igniters in moisture-proof containers, such as condoms or plastic sandwich bags. Damp or wet paper book matches will not ignite.

DRIED PEAS TIME-DELAY SWITCH

Note: All information contained in this book is presented for educational and informational purposes only. Many of the techniques are dangerous and should not be performed without training, proper supervision, and safety equipment, such as gloves, face mask, and eye protection. The authors, writers, editors, publisher, illustrator, and any other persons involved with this book are not liable for any damages, injuries, or legal actions that may arise from the use or misuse of any information contained herein. Always check the laws where you live and obey them. Don't do any harm and don't do any stupid stuff!

Make a time-delay device for an electrical firing circuit using the expansion of dried peas. What you'll need are dried peas, or other dehydrated seeds, a wide-mouth glass jar with a nonmetal cap, two screws or bolts, a thin metal plate, a hand drill, and a screwdriver.

1. Determine the time-delay experiment with the dried seeds to see how fast they raise. Most dried seeds increase about 50 percent in volume in one to two hours.
2. Cut a disc from the thin metal plate. It should fit loosely inside the jar. If the metal is painted or rusted, it must be scraped or sanded to obtain a clean metal surface.
3. Drill two holes in the jar about two inches apart. The diameter of the holes should match the size of the screws. Thread the screws (or bolts) tightly into the lid. If the jar has a metal cap, a piece of wood or plastic (not metal) can be used as a cover.
4. Pour dried seeds into the container. The level will depend on the previously measured rise time for the desired delay.
5. Place the metal disc in the jar on top of the seeds.
6. Add just enough water to completely cover the seeds and place the cap on the jar.
7. Attach connecting wires from the firing circuit to the two screws on the cap.
8. The expansion of the scenes will raise the metal disc until it contacts the screws and closes the circuit to cause the explosion.

No. 094: Dried Peas Time-Delay Switch

CONOP: The rehydration of dried peas can be used to trigger a time-delay device.

COA1: Acquire dried peas, or other dehydrated seeds, a wide mouth glass jar with a non-metal cap, two screws or bolts, a thin metal plate, a hand drill, and a screwdriver.

Non metallic lid

COA2: Cut a disc from the thin metal plate. It should fit loosely inside the jar. If the metal is painted or rusted, it must be scraped or sanded to obtain a clean metal surface.

COA3: Drill two holes in the jar about 2 inches apart. The diameter of the holes should match the size of the screws. Thread the screws (or bolts) tightly into the lid.

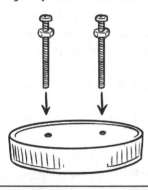

COA4: Pour dried seeds into the container and place the metal disc in the jar on top of the seeds.

Metallic lid
Dried peas

COA5: Add just enough water to completely cover the seeds and place the cap on the jar.

COA6: Attach connecting wires from the firing circuit to the two screws on the cap.

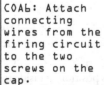

BLUF: Water temperature will affect the rate of expansion, so run experiments to accurately set the time delay.

NO. 095

TREMBLER SWITCH

Note: All information contained in this book is presented for educational and informational purposes only. Many of the techniques are dangerous and should not be performed without training, proper supervision, and safety equipment, such as gloves, face mask, and eye protection. The authors, writers, editors, publisher, illustrator, and any other persons involved with this book are not liable for any damages, injuries, or legal actions that may arise from the use or misuse of any information contained herein. Always check the laws where you live and obey them. Don't do any harm and don't do any stupid stuff!

Use a $2 ballpoint pen to anonymously trigger a bridge explosion while a tank or armored vehicle is passing overhead.

Main battle tanks weigh upward of forty-five tons and cause bridges to vibrate as they cross. An improvised trembler switch allows the saboteur to place the explosive and be miles away before the explosion. Depending on how sensitively the trembler has been set, the vibration will trigger the explosion whenever the next tank crosses the bridge.

You'll need a ballpoint pen spring, stiff copper wire, assorted small pieces of wood or plastic, insulated small gauge wire, a nail (with a flat head), some steel wool, and liquid solder.

1. Make an L-bracket out of two pieces of thin wood or plastic.
2. Glue the spring to the base and solder one lead of the wire to the bottom of the spring. Clean the spring with steel wool for good contacts.
3. Solder the nail vertically to the top of the spring.
4. Drill a small hole in the vertical side of the bracket and mount the copper wire through it. One end should be directly above the spring and formed into a half-inch circle.
5. Pull the nail directly up so that it stretches the spring about three inches and the nail is positioned inside the center of the copper loop.

Clamp the trembler to the bridge and connect the two leads into the firing circuit. When any part of the nail contacts the copper wire, the explosion will be triggered.

No. 095: Build a Trembler Switch

CONOP: Sabotage a bridge just as a tank or heavy truck is passing overhead.

COA1: Acquire a ballpoint pen spring, stiff copper wire, assorted small pieces of wood or plastic, insulated small gage wire, a nail (with a flat head), some steel wool, and liquid solder.

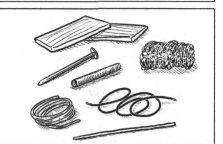

COA2: Make an L-bracket out of two pieces of thin wood or plastic

COA 3: Glue the spring to the base and solder one lead of the wire to the bottom of the spring. Clean the spring with steel wool for a good contact.

COA4: Solder the nail vertically to the top of the spring.

COA5: Drill a small hole in the vertical side of the bracket and mount the copper wire through it. One end should be directly above the spring and formed into a ½" circle

COA6: Pull the nail directly up so that it stretches the spring about three inches and the nail is positioned inside the center of the copper loop.

COA7: Connect the two leads into the firing circuit.

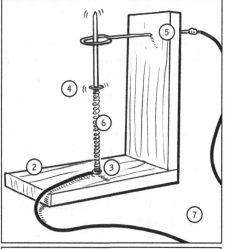

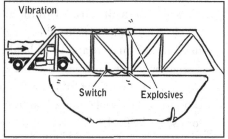

Vibration

Switch   Explosives

BLUF: Be long gone when it goes off.

SMOKE BOMBS

Smoke has tactical and signaling applications that are used to create a dense cloud of smoke in a specific area for various purposes. Once activated, the smoke emits a thick, colorful cloud that can obscure vision and provide concealment for troops or indicate wind direction and tactical information.

Smoke has several tactical uses, including providing concealment on the battlefield, creating confusion in a tactical situation, and signaling a position or location to other units. They are used by military forces, law enforcement agencies, and firefighters to obscure vision and obscure targets during operations. Smoke can also be used in civilian settings for signaling rescue teams, providing distraction and cover, or signaling distress.

Combine three tablespoons of potassium nitrate and two tablespoons of sugar and pour into the skillet. Stir the mixture for fifteen minutes over medium heat until the sugar caramelizes and the dark colored mixture looks like caramel. Add one tablespoon of baking soda into the mix before you take it off the heat. Try not to create bubbles or air pockets as you stir, and don't overcook and let the mixture catch on fire! Also be certain to wear a mask and avoid inhaling the fumes.

If you want to produce colored smoke, add a tablespoon of colored organic dye into the mix in the skillet. You can produce colored smoke in a variety of bright colors.

Create a small "boat" with the aluminum foil and pour the mixture into it to harden. Try to avoid leaving any air pockets. Insert a three-inch fuse into the mixture and let in harden for an hour. Then wrap it up like a small burrito leaving only the fuse exposed.

Mark the outside of the foil to indicate the color of the smoke. You can produce multiple smoke bombs in advance and carry them with you for use in the field.

When smoke is needed, light the fuse and throw the bomb into an open area. Be careful since this mix burns at a very high temperature and produces a jet of flame as it burns.

No. 096: Smoke Bombs

CONOP: Smoke bombs can be used to make you either visible, or invisible.

COA1: Gather your ingredients: sugar, saltpeter, baking soda, tinfoil, fuses, and a cast iron skillet.

COA2: Combine three tablespoons of saltpeter and two tablespoons of sugar. Add organic dye if you would like colored smoke. Stir the mixture in a cast iron skillet for the dark colored mixture looks like caramel.

COA3: Pour the mixture into a tinfoil "boat" and insert a 3" fuse before it hardens. Allow it to solidify for one hour and wrap tightly with foil.

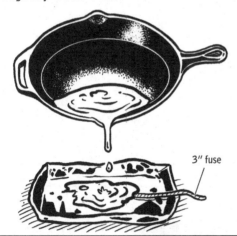

3" fuse

COA4: Add a tablespoon of colored organic dye into the mix and mark each of your smoke bombs with the color of smoke.

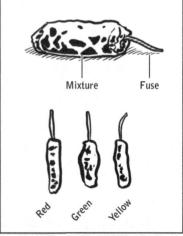

Mixture   Fuse

Red   Green   Yellow

BLUF: Disappearing in a puff of smoke may save your life.

For informational purposes only,
exercise caution, prioritize safety, and obey all laws.

Be certain to wear safety gear including latex gloves and a filter mask, and have proper ventilation and supervision.

Note: All information contained in this book is presented for educational and informational purposes only. Many of the techniques are dangerous and should not be performed without training, proper supervision, and safety equipment, such as gloves, face mask, and eye protection. The authors, writers, editors, publisher, illustrator, and any other persons involved with this book are not liable for any damages, injuries, or legal actions that may arise from the use or misuse of any information contained herein. Always check the laws where you live and obey them. Don't do any harm and don't do any stupid stuff!

NO. 097

ANTIDRONE SHELLS

Enemy reconnaissance drones pose an ominous threat to fighters by spotting targets and feeding location data to weapons systems that will try to kill you. Fortunately, most consumer-level drones are quite fragile and almost anything that hits them or touches them is likely to cause them to crash or lose orientation. A long-barrel twelve-gauge shotgun with a tight choke and firing number 4 or number 5 shot is a viable solution for drones flying within one hundred yards. However, drones are very elusive, and you should always lead a moving target.

A better alternative is to create custom twelve-gauge antidrone shells that will expand and slice a drone in half. Here's how:

1. Remove existing buckshot from a 00 twelve-gauge buckshot shell.
2. Take six of the 00 lead balls and drill a hole in each large enough for the wire to pass through twice.
3. Loop a single strand of copper wire through and back around through (again) each ball. Separate each ball with three inches of wire. No knots are used.
4. Coil the wire between balls and gently load them back into the shell.
5. The light weight of the balls will propel them at over 1600 feet per second.
6. Add a rifle choke to the shotgun, or use a rifled barrel, to increase rotation and cause the balls to spread. The purpose of the wire is simply to control the spread and concentrate the power of the shot.

Note: All information contained in this book is presented for educational and informational purposes only. Many of the techniques are dangerous and should not be performed without training, proper supervision, and safety equipment, such as gloves, face mask, and eye protection. The authors, writers, editors, publisher, illustrator, and any other persons involved with this book are not liable for any damages, injuries, or legal actions that may arise from the use or misuse of any information contained herein. Always check the laws where you live and obey them. Don't do any harm and don't do any stupid stuff!

For informational purposes only, exercise caution, prioritize safety, and obey all laws.

No. 097: Anti-Drone Shotgun Shells

CONOP: Small reconnaissance drones are an increasing danger on the battlefield.

COA1: Remove 00 buckshot from a 12 gauge shotgun shell.

COA2: Drill a hole in each lead ball large enough for the wire to pass through twice. Separate each round by three inches of wire.

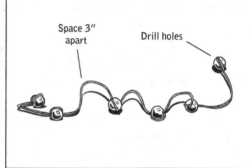

Space 3" apart

Drill holes

COA3: Coil the wire between balls and gently load them back into the shell.

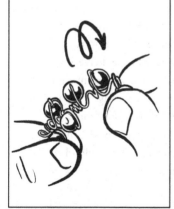

COA4: Maintain a 24-hour watch for drones with a shooter and a spotter using a powerful flashlight.

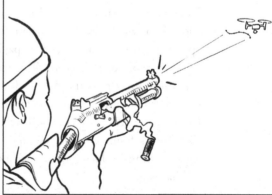

BLUF: Kill the drone before the drone kills you.

For informational purposes only,
exercise caution, prioritize safety, and obey all laws.

DRONE DROP SYSTEM

Over the past decade, drones have increasingly become popular on the battlefield. They have revolutionized warfare by providing real-time reconnaissance, surveillance, and target identification capabilities to military forces. The use of drones has significantly reduced the risk to human lives by enabling the military to gather intelligence and strike targets from a safer distance. Drones can also operate in dangerous areas and at high altitudes that are not accessible by manned aircraft. As a result, they have become a valuable tool for military operations, including counterterrorism, search and rescue, and reconnaissance missions. The popularity of drones on the battlefield is expected to continue to grow as technology advances and drones become more automated and less expensive to manufacture.

Here is a basic outline for building a drop system for a drone:

1. Choose the type of delivery mechanism. There are several options for delivering payloads from a drone, including gravity-based systems, mechanical release mechanisms, and magnetic drop systems.

2. Design the payload container. Ensure that the container is sturdy enough to withstand the flight and landing conditions and is appropriately sized for the type of payload you are delivering.

3. Mount the payload container. This could involve mounting the container directly to the drone's frame or creating a separate mechanism for attaching and detaching it from the drone.

4. Control the release mechanism. This could involve programming the drone's flight control system to release the payload at a specific time or location or incorporating a remote release mechanism.

No. 098: Drone Drop

CONOP: Small "hobbyist" drones may be controlled by individual soldiers or groups of ground forces, and employed to scout the battleground or as weaponry.

COA1: Acquire Supplies:

Personal drone (DGI Mavic)

Grenade

Empty tube

String

Zip ties

COA4: Zip tie Tube to drone and attach the string to a fixed portion of the drone

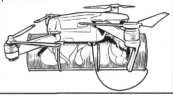

COA5: Hover drone over target. Flair drone to let grenade slide out towards the target.

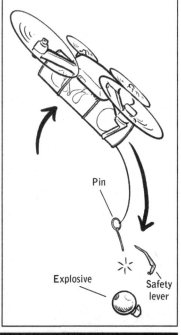

Pin

Explosive

Safety lever

COA2: Attach string to grenade pin and straighten the prongs

Straighten stab to easily slip out.

Attach String to other end.

COA3: Place grenade upright in tube with the string hanging out

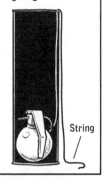

String

BLUF: An invader's greatest fear is death from above.

For informational purposes only,
exercise caution, prioritize safety, and obey all laws.

5. Test the drop system. Conduct multiple test flights to verify that the drop system is functioning properly and that the payload is being delivered safely and accurately.
6. Optimize the system. Based on the results of the test flights, make any necessary adjustments to improve the performance and reliability of the drop system.

This is a high-level outline, and the specific details of the implementation will depend on the type of drone and delivery mechanism you choose as well as the specific requirements of your application.

NO. 099

TETHERED DRONE

Using a small drone like the DJI Mini 2 tethered to a power source will give you hours of sustained drone surveillance without having to service the drone or change batteries for long periods of time.

Leveraging a drone for force protection operations allows constant eye in the sky monitoring, ensuring your adversaries are not sneaking up on your location. The drones can also be self-contained tethered to a golf cart battery and then monitored from afar as to not give up the monitoring location. Running multiple tethered drones will inevitably give you the situational awareness needed to survive in an urban or rural combat environment.

Tethering your drone to a golf cart battery requires some simple pieces of gear. You will need one hundred feet of twenty-two-gauge DC power cable, eight-volt golf cart battery, soldering, iron, and resin. You can use maritime batteries as well, but if the battery exceeds eight volts, then a voltage regulator will be required.

First break the plastic molding around the battery off to reveal the leads attached to the female receptacle outlet. After the leads are separated, solder the bitter end of the twenty-two-gauge cable to the leads. Ensure that you're connecting positive to positive and negative to negative. Connect the other bitter end of the twenty-two-gauge cable positive to positive terminal and negative terminal.

Once everything is connected, plug the female outlet into the drone's male outlet and your drone should power on. Turn on drone and ascend to seventy-five feet, allowing twenty-five feet of flexibility, and the drone should sustain flight for twelve-plus hours.

No. 099: Tethered Drone

CONOP: Use amateur drones to provide constant and consistent overwatch.

COA1: Acquire Materials

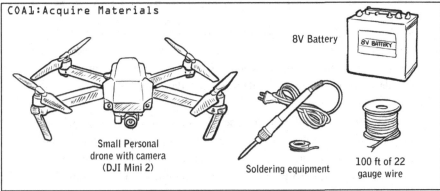

8V Battery

Small Personal
drone with camera
(DJI Mini 2)

Soldering equipment

100 ft of 22
gauge wire

COA2: Remove battery from drone.

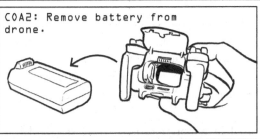

COA3: Take apart the plastic battery housing and disconnect the battery. Connect the Positive and negative leads to the 22 Ga wire.

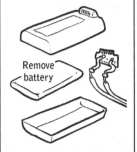

Remove
battery

COA4: Connect the other end of the wire to the 8V battery.

COA5: Reconnect battery housing and insert back in drone. Fly the drone for 12+ hours.

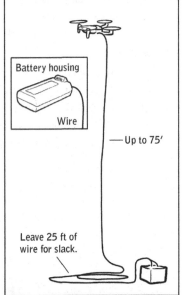

Battery housing

Wire

—Up to 75'

Leave 25 ft of
wire for slack.

BLUF: The eye in the sky never sleeps.

COVERT LANDING STRIP

Covert airstrips are essential for military operations since they enable the military to fly aircraft into and out of strategic regions without being detected or hampered by the enemy. Covert airstrips are required when standard airfields are not available or too dangerous to use due to the enemy's capabilities.

Covert airfield offers a surprise advantage to military forces. It can help to catch the enemy off guard by allowing military aircraft to land and take off undetected. Covert airfields can be made in areas that are far from expected enemy lines, thus allowing quick infiltration of troops behind enemy lines.

Covert airfields offer strategic advantages over the enemy. The stealthy approach to the enemy's location while avoiding established airfields can make it challenging for the enemy to anticipate the direction of an attack. It can also divert the enemy's attention away from the main objectives, allowing the military to achieve their desired results without the enemy's knowledge.

Covert airfields can be used in remote locations where standard airports are not operational. For remote operations, the construction of a standard airport may not be feasible due to the financial, security, and logistical constraints. Therefore, a covert airfield can be used as an alternative solution to bringing in the required military supplies, personnel, and equipment.

No. 100: Covert Landing Strip

CONOP: Covert landing strips are useful for both INFILS (infiltrations) and EXFILS (exfiltrations).

COA1: Measure out your landing strip and remove any obstacles.

Start of runway

End of runway

1,500 ft

COA2: Create the box pattern with four lights and dig the holes.

x3 Plastic trash bags

Rubber band

Infrared

Direction of plane

Dig holes to allow the flash lights to be buried at 45°.

COA3: Place a single light on a stick to mark the end of the runway. Point it facing the landing aircraft.

COA4: Remove all traces from landing site.

BLUF: Keep the engine running while you load/unload for a quick turnaround.

For informational purposes only,
exercise caution, prioritize safety, and obey all laws.

ABOUT THE AUTHOR

Clint Emerson is a retired U.S. Navy SEAL with over 20 years of service, a New York Times best-selling author, and crisis management professional. Throughout his military career, he served in various combat zones executing high-stakes missions including against Somali Pirates, AQ Leaders, and other covert operations. As a operative within the elite group known as SEAL Team 6, Clint developed a strong foundation in intelligence collection, surveillance, and singleton operations.

Upon retiring from the Navy, Clint's passion for empowering others with lifesaving skills led him to create the '100 Deadly Skills' book series. By sharing his unique background and extensive knowledge, he provides readers with strategies to help protect themselves in dangerous or potentially life-threatening situations.

As the founder of Escape the Wolf, a crisis management consultancy dedicated to addressing risk for corporations and organizations, his distinguished background and relevant experiences make him a sought-after speaker and trainer for various organizations, including government agencies and private corporations. Clint is dedicated to promoting safety and educating the public by providing actionable information, emphasizing the importance of personal preparedness and resilience. His work has been featured in various media outlets, including numerous television appearances, podcasts, and articles.

Printed in the United States
by Baker & Taylor Publisher Services